INSIDE THE MINDS

Privacy and Surveillance Legal Issues

Leading Lawyers on Navigating Changes in Security Program Requirements and Helping Clients Prevent Breaches

ASPATORE

For additional copies or customer service inquiries, please e-mail west.customer.service@thomson.com.

ISBN 978-0-314-29174-5

Mat #41596246

CONTENTS

Demonstrating Due Diligence in Building an Information Security Program

Cheryl A. Falvey

Partner

Crowell & Moring LLP

ASPATORE

Introduction: Risk Assessment

A risk assessment represents a critical first step for a sound information security program. It also provides evidence that the organization took the time to identify vulnerabilities and address them, which can prove useful down the road, particularly in the event of a breach. While a variety of information security standards exist in the public and private sectors, nearly all include a risk assessment as an essential building block in the security process. Given my experience in the government sector, I look to the National Institute of Standards and Technology (NIST) information security standards that include risk assessments as a fundamental component of a cybersecurity program.[1] In its standards, NIST lays out a six-step framework for a structured risk assessment. Some of the relevant considerations may include the following:

- What are your information technology (IT) network boundaries? The risks are larger in companies with many offices spread across international boundaries with many devices (laptops, tablets, smartphones, and devices from home).
- What data do you store and exchange? In the event of a breach, the company can be flat-footed if it does not have a good accounting of what confidential information it housed and where.
- Who is inside your network boundary? Companies with business partners with direct access to their internal network face a greater threat. Limiting the access to sensitive data both internally and to external business partners can minimize the risk of loss.
- What are your security controls? Knowing the levels of security controls necessary for what different types of information can help tailor those controls to the biggest risks. Medical records and documents with names and addresses need more protection than those that do not contain confidential information.
- Are your risks static? Auditing risk levels that may vary over time as equipment purchases increase or policies change will help manage risks. A new bring-your-own device policy or increase in international

[1] NIST Special Publication (SP) 800-39, *Managing Information Security Risk* (Mar. 2011); NIST SP 800-37, Rev. 1, *Guide for Applying the Risk Management Framework to Federal Information Systems* (Feb. 2010).

travel can change the risk profile significantly. Security controls must adapt to the changing threat environment.

While just a summary of the much more detailed NIST standards for a risk management framework, these factors help develop a cybersecurity program that meets the specific business needs.

Enforcing the Security Program

The NIST standards also contain extensive detail for enforcing the security program.[2] Some of the key elements include the following.

- *Training.* Training is not only required,[3] but essential to an effective security program. Many security threats inflict injury, not due to a gap in the technical controls, but because of social engineering (*e.g.*, someone clicked on a bad website and brought back a virus). Every employee, from the top down, should participate in yearly training as a best practice to demonstrate a true commitment to the security program.
- *Monitoring.* The security program must be tested, monitored, and updated for security threats.[4] As discussed earlier, continuous monitoring involves a real-time monitoring and updating process to defend against rapidly evolving and escalating threats.
- *Accountability.* A security program requires that personnel must be held accountable for following the security rules.[5]
- *Incident Detection and Reporting.* When the security defenses are breached, an organization must have a way to detect the breach and a method for reporting it.[6]

Security measures must be ingrained in your business processes and culture. In the government, if you used an unencrypted thumb drive or USB device, someone from the IT group arrived at your door within minutes. That

[2] NIST SP 800-53, Rev. 4, Apr. 2013, http://csrc.nist.gov/publications/drafts/800-53-rev4/sp800-53-rev4-ipd.pdf.
[3] 44 U.S.C. § 3544(b)(4) (2002).
[4] 44 U.S.C. § 3544(a)(2)(D).
[5] 44 U.S.C. § 3544(a)(3)(A).
[6] 44 U.S.C. § 3544(b)(7).

demonstrates both monitoring and accountability. In fact, we had been so sensitized to the fact that even the use of a unencrypted thumb drive could present a security risk that we stopped a meeting with Chinese government representatives until we could have the device with their Power Point scanned before it was used.

In the private sector, companies must conduct risk assessments and enforce security measures to meet the standard of care. The Federal Trade Commission (FTC) has committed to aggressively pursue companies that do not secure consumer data and ensure that computer systems cannot be hacked. In a recent settlement of a case the FTC brought against TrendNet, Inc. for failing to secure camera feeds used for baby monitoring, the Commission ordered that the firm employ NIST-like compliance measures to safeguard against intrusion. The consent decree ordered that the firm:

- Designate an employee responsible for the security program;
- Identify all material internal and external security risks throughout each area of operation, including employee training and management, product and software design and development;
- Review and assess third party vulnerabilities and penetration risks and response capabilities;
- Safeguard systems with testing and monitoring, including architecture and code reviews.

The terms of the order recognize the need to continually reassess systems and vulnerabilities over time and require evaluation and adjustment in light of the required testing and monitoring activities. These types of requirements are the new normal used to meet the standard of care.

Risk and Security Concerns Vary By Industry: Legal Industry Example

Different industries can have very different risk profiles, depending on the nature of their business. A company engaging directly with the public on the Internet may have more vulnerabilities than a company with a closed network structure and only a public-facing web site. However, no matter the industry, everyone is susceptible to a cyber attack and the consequences of a network disruption.

Interestingly, the legal profession itself has been forced to make cybersecurity a major priority, given the confidential client documentation they both keep and create. On November 1, 2009, the FBI issued an advisory warning to law firms that they were specifically being targeted by hackers. Increasingly, hackers have looked to law firms as a backdoor into their clients' most valuable secrets. As the assistant general counsel of Bank of America warned, law firms are "considered one of the biggest vectors that the hackers, or others, are going to go at to try to get to our information."[7] One of the more widely reported security breaches occurred in the midst of an unsuccessful attempt to close a $40 billion corporate acquisition:

> China-based cyber thieves, for instance, hacked into the computer networks of seven law firms in 2010 to get more information about BHP Billiton Ltd.'s ultimately unsuccessful $40 billion bid to acquire Canadian company Potash Corp. of Saskatchewan, Inc., Bloomberg reported in January.[8]

American Bar Association (ABA) Immediate Past President Laurel Bellows made law firm cybersecurity a priority for 2012-13.[9] The ABA passed a resolution in August 2013 condemning unauthorized and illegal intrusions into the computers systems and networks utilized by lawyers. It also urged lawyers to review and comply with the provisions in the Model Rules of Professional Conduct for lawyers regarding safe guarding confidential client information. Based upon the magnitude of the risks and the recognized ethical obligations, hardly anyone would argue that lawyers need not worry about cybersecurity. The more difficult question is what lawyers should do about it. A number of books and articles have provided guidance and recommended best practices for law firm cybersecurity, including several works by the ABA.[10] Training programs designed to increase awareness of

---

[7] Catherine Dunn, *Outside Law Firm Cybersecurity Under Scrutiny*, CORPORATE COUNSEL, Jun. 6, 2013.

[8] B. Elgin, D. Lawrence & M. Riley, *Coke Gets Hacked and Doesn't Tell Anyone*, BLOOMBERG, Nov. 4, 2012, http://www.bloomberg.com/news/2012-11-04/coke-hacked-and-doesn-t-tell.html.

[9] James Podgers, *Raising the Alarm*, 99 ABA J. 55 (2013).

[10] *See, e.g.*, SHARON D. NELSON, JOHN W. SIMEK, & DAVID G. RIES, LOCKED DOWN: INFORMATION SECURITY FOR LAWYERS (ABA Section of Law Practice Management, 2012); Judge Herbert B. Dixon, Jr., *Cybersecurity...How Important Is It?*, 51 JUDGES J. 36 (2012).

the risks and identifying matters from the start that may involve the collection of sensitive data are ways lawyers can build business practices to prevent security breach.

Risks and Security Concerns for Different Types of Data

Determining which of the many laws that apply to data privacy breaches can turn not just on the industry, but also the information or data at issue. The type of data being kept can affect the regulatory obligation to protect the information and to report any security breach. For example, the Health Information Technology for Economic and Clinical Health Act (HITECH) requires certain Internet-based businesses to notify consumers regarding a breach of protected electronic health information. Different regulators may need to be engaged depending on the type of information that has been accessed. Generally speaking, however, most states now require some sort of notification when "personal information" has been obtained using unauthorized means." The definition of personally protected information can vary slightly from state to state but often includes the person's name and one additional piece of information such as social security number, driver's license number, or credit card information. Knowing what data should be kept confidential can help a company identify what security controls are needed as well as who needs to be contacted in the event of a breach. Classifying the data by level of confidentiality, sensitivity, and even whether it falls under a specific statutory obligation can go a long way toward managing a breach event. It can also help a company build security practices into their business operating procedures. If HIPPA-protected medical data is flagged as such from the point at which it is created, it will be easier to catalogue and protect that information than to do so outside of the normal business process.

Helping Clients with Compliance

Lawyers can help their clients identify what data they are legally required to protect and keep confidential. They can also assist with the review of contracts to clarify what data the company is bound to protect contractually. Lawyers can help identify insurance coverage issues and ensure that everything required to keep that coverage in place is being done in accordance with the coverage terms. A lawyer's knowledge of the security breach notification laws is essential, but in the event of a breach, a lawyer can also assist with the crisis communications, interfacing with law enforcement and any government or internal investigation. Engaging in a mock breach exercise can help the company identify all that will need to be done in the event of a security breach. Individuals can be assigned responsibility for contacting state regulators, credit reporting agencies, and form documents can be drafted to aid in increasing response time. It can be difficult to act promptly if the company is scrambling to identify what notification requirements they must follow and who they need to contact in the middle of a crisis.

Benefits of a Solid Compliance and Ethics Program

The goal of any compliance and ethics program is twofold: (1) to ensure that the company complies with all applicable regulatory requirements, such as the reporting requirements under HIPPA, and (2) to avoid prosecution to the extent possible, should the company be faced with an issue of noncompliance.

The most practical return on investment is by conducting a risk assessment and building a compliance program in compliance with the law. Most states generically require "appropriate administrative, technical, and physical security safeguards." Additionally, a compliance program helps create a defense to a claim of a regulatory violation, or a class action complaint alleging that the company did not exercise reasonable care in the maintenance and control of information. A successful compliance program must have support from the highest levels of management. The ownership of compliance obligations must sit with high-level managers who have the resources to carry out compliance and who are evaluated on that success equally with their other job expectations.

The future of security is confounded by the plethora of consumer products that now employ technology and access the Internet as a routine part of their operation. We can change our thermostat and turn on our lights with our mobile devices. The FTC emphasizes a recurring theme of the need to keep commercial data practices transparent and for the companies that make these products to secure the data they use and collect. This interconnectivity of devices and products, now known as the "Internet of Things," presents the next data protection challenge.

Conclusion

Every business using the Internet to conduct its business must use risk assessment to meet the standard of care required to ensure that data is adequately protected. In the event of an unauthorized intrusion, advanced preparation will ensure rapid response to minimize any potential harm to consumers. Having a team trained to respond to incidents before they happen and knowing what sensitive data is being stored, and is potentially at risk, will pay dividends in the event of a security breach.

Key Takeaways

- A risk assessment represents a critical first step for a sound information security program.
- No matter the industry, everyone is susceptible to a cyber attack and the consequences of a network disruption.
- The legal profession itself has been forced to make cybersecurity a major priority, given the confidential client documentation they both keep and create. Increasingly, hackers have looked to law firms as a backdoor into their clients' most valuable secrets.
- Lawyers can help their clients identify what data they are legally required to protect and keep confidential. They can also assist with the review of contracts to clarify what data the company is bound to protect contractually.

Cheryl A. Falvey is a partner in Crowell & Moring LLP's Washington, DC office. Ms. Falvey provides litigation and counseling services, with a focus on consumer protection matters, including product safety, privacy, sweepstakes, promotions, and advertising. Ms. Falvey concentrates on the defense of consumer class action, toxic tort, mass tort, and other tort claims arising out of consumer, occupational, and environmental exposures, as well as trade secret, intellectual property, and other technology litigation, representing clients in the food and beverage, consumer product, technology, energy and chemical industry sectors.

Ms. Falvey began counseling clients on security breach issues when California passed the first breach notification law. During her tenure as the general counsel of the US Consumer Product Safety Commission, she supervised the lawyers handling privacy compliance in the agency and advised and approved agency policies designed to identify confidential information and protect it against security breach and network hacking.

Acknowledgment: *Special thanks are due to my colleagues for their key contributions: Dazid Z. Bodenheimer, Kerry Mustico, Elliot Golding, Kate Molony, and Gordon Griffin.*

The Information Governance Approach to Privacy and Data Security Compliance

Peter Sloan

Partner

Husch Blackwell LLP

ASPATORE

Introduction

Compliance with US privacy and data security laws is a daunting task for companies today. The depth and breadth of requirements at the federal and state levels continue to expand. At the same time, the manner in which companies create, receive, use, store, and transmit information is rapidly evolving. Yesterday's challenge was the protection and management of accumulating volumes of information primarily contained within the company's firewalls and other perimeters. Today, the information is still accumulating, and at an accelerating pace. The additional challenge is that the perimeter walls have all but fallen, with information flowing in and out of companies more freely than ever before through such phenomena as cloud computing and expansion of service provider arrangements.

Companies must adapt, finding new strategies to apply existing compliance requirements to a complex, evolving information environment. This chapter offers the proposition that effective privacy and data security compliance in today's environment compels companies to adopt an information governance approach to managing their information.

Information Governance

Information governance is a company's *integrated approach* to complying with information-related requirements and controlling information-related risks.

It is an *approach* because information governance is a strategic response by the company to an information environment in which costs, exposures, and opportunities arise in interrelated ways, not only for the privacy and security of protected information, but also regarding retention and lifecycle management of information and also the preservation and production of relevant information in litigation. At any given moment, the same information may be covered by privacy and data security requirements, be subject to records retention and information management requirements, and be under a preservation duty in pending or impending litigation. This is indeed a complex, interconnected compliance environment. In light of the attendant risks and costs, such an environment demands a strategic, systematic response from the company.

Information governance is an *integrated* approach because, in this complex information environment, companies must satisfy and reconcile what is required in at least three information-related disciplines: privacy and data security, records and information management, and litigation preservation and discovery. These disciplines have often been pursued by companies in an autonomous way, with each discipline developing its own tools and processes in relative isolation. In fact, these disciplines are so disconnected that their terminology is often foreign to each other. For example, to an e-discovery specialist, *OCR* clearly means optical character recognition, but to a privacy officer, *OCR* is obviously the Health and Human Services (HHS) Office of Civil Rights, responsible for enforcing Health Insurance Portability and Accountability Act (HIPAA) compliance. While a records and information management professional understands that source data ends up being stored in a *data repository*, an e-discovery specialist views the ultimate data storage location as a *data source.*

As a result, those responsible for privacy and data security often make decisions about information without full consideration of the repercussions for lifecycle management of the information or for e-discovery; the IT department and those handling paper records management tend to make decisions about information without full appreciation of cost and exposure repercussions for either privacy and data security or litigation discovery; and so forth. Inefficiency and duplication of resources are the result, as those pursuing these respective disciplines often fail to take full advantage of the efforts of others. More ominously, decisions made by one discipline may cause unintended problems and complications from the perspectives of the other disciplines. For lack of an integrated approach, such companies inevitably incur unnecessary risk and expense.

In contrast, companies pursuing an information governance approach integrate their thinking and actions regarding information across these various disciplines. Such companies seek to understand the full range of information compliance requirements and risks that arise from privacy and data security obligations, lifecycle records and information management, and litigation. They then establish information policies, processes, and controls designed in a balanced way to satisfy compliance requirements and control information risks arising from this full range of issues. They duly consider this integrated compliance and risk environment when making decisions of consequence regarding information.

Applying Information Governance to Privacy and Data Security Compliance

The wide range of privacy and data security compliance requirements under US federal and state laws generally divides into three categories: data security safeguards, breach notification, and privacy policies and notifications.

First, covered organizations must provide data security for the information protected under the particular legal scheme, with adequate administrative, physical, technical, and organizational safeguards. Thus, under HIPAA (as expanded by the Health Information Technology for Economic and Clinical Health [HITECH] Act), covered entities and their business associates must ensure the confidentiality, integrity, and availability of all electronic protected health information (ePHI) they create, receive, maintain, or transmit in compliance with HIPAA security standards for administrative, physical, and technical safeguards.[1] Financial institutions under the Gramm-Leach-Bliley Act must protect nonpublic personal information about their customers by developing and implementing a written comprehensive information security program containing appropriate administrative, technical, and physical safeguards.[2] Data security requirements are also embedded in a wide range of federal privacy laws applicable to organizations generally, such as regulations under the Family Medical Leave Act (FMLA), the Americans With Disabilities Act (ADA), and the Genetic Information Nondiscrimination Act (GINA), as well as in the Occupational Safety and Health Administration (OSHA) and Department of Transportation (DOT) regulations. At least nine states (Arkansas, California, Maryland, Massachusetts, Nevada, Oregon, Rhode Island, Texas, and Utah) require organizations with personally identifiable information (PII) of state residents to implement and maintain reasonable security procedures and practices to protect such PII from unauthorized access, destruction, use, modification, or disclosure. The Massachusetts regulatory scheme is the most exacting, requiring such entities to implement both a comprehensive information security program with administrative, technical, and physical safeguards, and also an information

[1] *See* 45 C.F.R.§ 164, subpart C.
[2] *See, e.g.*, 16 C.F.R. § 314.3(a)&(b) (Federal Trade Commission Safeguards Rules).

security program with specified data security protections.[3] A majority of states have laws requiring organizations with PII to take reasonable measures to protect such information when it is disposed of or discarded. Some such states require organizations to have a destruction policy, while others specify the means of disposal for PII, such as shredding of hardcopy documents, effective erasure of electronic media, or other actions to render the PII unreadable or indecipherable.

Second, various federal and state laws mandate security breach notification. Under HIPAA/HITECH, covered entities and their business associates must make required notifications if the security or privacy of PHI is compromised through acquisition, access, use, or disclosure in a manner not permitted under the HIPAA Privacy Rules.[4] State law commonly requires organizations possessing PII of states' residents to notify such residents if there is a breach of security regarding their PII. Virtually every state (except Alabama, Kentucky, New Mexico, and South Dakota) has such a law, and the Texas law provides that persons conducting business in Texas must also provide breach notification for residents of states that do not have their own breach notification laws.[5]

Third, privacy laws commonly require organizations possessing protected information to provide to the affected individuals notification of the organization's privacy policies for protection of such information, often with related requirements for opt-out or consent regarding information-related practices and transactions. For example, HIPAA/HITECH requires covered entities and business associates to comply with privacy standards covering, among other matters, privacy policies and disclosure consent.[6] Regulations under the Gramm-Leach-Bliley Act mandate that financial institutions provide customers notice of their privacy policies regarding the protection of customer information, and also include requirements for opt-out notifications and mechanisms.[7]

It is of course possible for a company to pursue these three elements of privacy and data security compliance in an isolated, stand-alone manner, without

---

[3] *See* 201 C.M.R. 17.03-04 (West).
[4] *See* 35 C.F.R. § 164, subpart D (West).
[5] Tex. Bus. & Com. Code Ann. § 521.053 (West).
[6] *See* 45 C.F.R. § 164, subpart E.
[7] *See, e.g.*, 16 C.F.R. § 313 (Federal Trade Commission Privacy Rules).

coordinating with the company's other information-focused disciplines. That is precisely what many companies have attempted, yielding mixed results. However, with an information governance approach, the company's privacy and data security efforts are more likely to be successful due to synergies with other information-related disciplines, such as records and information management and litigation preservation and discovery. The points below illustrate how companies that pursue information governance as a strategic imperative can realize, among other benefits, more robust compliance with privacy and data security requirements. If one visualizes information compliance and risk control as a stool, it is poorly supported by the single leg of privacy and data security. Instead, information compliance and risk control are more soundly and sturdily buttressed by three, interconnected legs: the disciplines of privacy and data security, records and information management, and litigation preservation and discovery.

Synergies of the information governance approach for privacy and data security compliance include the following:

1. *Protected Information Clarity.* Privacy and data security compliance is more effective when the company has clarity about precisely what protected information is in its possession or control, the physical location of such information, the type of storage media used for such information throughout its life cycle, and the identity of the internal function or role that has stewardship responsibility for the information. For example, in breach response efforts, it becomes crucial to understand what (if any) protected information resided in a lost or stolen laptop or back-up data storage device. Awareness of what information exists, where, in what media, and under whose stewardship is a hallmark of the records and information management discipline. By aligning privacy and data security processes with these traditional strengths of records and information management, the company benefits from a deeper and more accurate understanding of its protected information.
2. *Application of Privacy and Data Security Policies and Controls.* Privacy and data security policies are most effective when they can be effectively understood and applied by those handling protected information. Thus, instead of simply having a privacy and data security policy and a high-level data security matrix, companies using an information

governance approach can directly link their privacy and data security requirements to specific information types in the company's records retention schedule or other information classification framework. Thus, such companies can categorize their various records or information types and attach to them both records retention periods and also privacy and data security rules. In this way, the privacy and data security requirements become embedded in the file plans and other basic organizational structures that personnel use on a daily basis when handling the company's information.

Privacy and data security compliance is also more successful when information security controls can be applied directly to the specific paper and data systems, processes, and repositories in which protected information resides. Companies that have adopted the information governance approach can link together privacy and data security control requirements with their mapping of paper and electronic data repositories, thereby embedding privacy and security controls into such systems.

It is the records and information management discipline that provides to companies a more specific understanding of information classification structures, such as records retention schedules and file plans, and also mapping of paper and electronic data systems and repositories. By adopting an information governance approach, companies make it possible to directly attach privacy and data security rules to such classification schemes and information repositories, making compliance more efficient and more reliable.

3. *Disposal of Unnecessary Protected Information.* It is axiomatic that a company cannot suffer a breach of protected information that has already been compliantly and securely disposed of. Privacy and data security compliance is thus enhanced when organizations promptly and compliantly dispose of protected information that is no longer needed or required. Life cycle management of information, including timely disposal of unnecessary information, lies squarely within the discipline of records and information management. Companies that embrace information governance have the extra motivation of privacy and data

security compliance for systematically and appropriately disposing of unnecessary information, which, among other benefits, reduces the risk of protected information breaches.

4. *Beneficial Interplay with Litigation Processes.* Privacy and data security compliance benefits from coordination with the company's litigation processes, in many of the same ways discussed earlier in this chapter regarding the records and information management discipline. The litigation imperative of the preservation duty causes organizations to become aware of the existence and location of all information relevant to pending or impending litigation, beyond the scope of what the company treats as records in the ordinary course of business. This deeper and broader understanding of information in the company's possession, custody, or control can help companies apply privacy and data security rules to all information, even transitory or duplicative information that is often beyond the scope of traditional records management. Data mapping conducted by many companies to support the preservation and collection of electronically stored information (ESI) in litigation can also identify data repositories for protected information, to which privacy and data security rules and controls may then be applied. The tracking of information preserved or collected for litigation can be a useful tool for the company's privacy and data security function, helping to ensure that privacy and data security rules are applied to such information, which is outside the traditional scope of records and information management.
5. *Leadership Commitment.* In most companies today, the bandwidth of management attention and the availability of resources are limited. Though privacy and data security compliance is obviously important, those responsible for it within the company may experience difficulty in obtaining leadership commitment and adequate resources to support their compliance efforts. Adoption of the information governance approach, in contrast, elevates the issue to a higher strategic level for the company. Information governance, as an organizational, strategic approach to managing information as an asset to address information requirements and control information risks, may present as a more compelling matter, attracting a higher level of leadership attention, commitment, and support. Such engagement by

the company's leadership is essential for creating and sustaining a control environment for governing information. Companies with an effective control environment for compliance, featuring "tone at the top," are more likely to achieve their strategic compliance objectives.[8]

Information Governance in Action: Service Providers

A representative, concrete example of how information governance can enable better privacy and data security compliance is the expanding use of service providers to store or process a company's protected information. As noted earlier in this chapter, today's information environment features a flooding of information into and out of companies, largely due to cloud computing and other service provider relationships. The notion of controlling information by simple containment within the company's perimeter has essentially vanished, overcome by the pervasive flow of information across such boundaries. Yet privacy and data security requirements for protected information must still be satisfied in this free-flowing environment, and many such requirements squarely address service provider arrangements.

For example, HIPAA-covered entities and business associates that permit third parties to create, receive, maintain, or transmit ePHI on their behalf must obtain satisfactory assurances that the third party will appropriately safeguard the information as required, with the assurances documented in a written contract.[9] Such contracts must, among other matters, require the third party to:

- establish permitted and required uses and disclosures of PHI;[10]
- establish appropriate, compliant security safeguards for ePHI;[11]
- report to the covered entity any breaches of unsecured PHI, security incident, or other unauthorized use or disclosure of PHI;[12] and

---

[8] *See* COSO, Internal Control—Integrated Framework, Executive Summary, 3 (May 2013) ("Internal control is a process effected by an entity's board of directors, management, and other personnel, designed to provide reasonable assurance regarding the achievement of objectives relating to operations, reporting, and compliance.").

[9] 45 C.F.R. § 164.308(b) (West).

[10] 45 C.F.R. § 164.504(e)(2)(i) (West).

[11] 45 C.F.R. § 164.314(a)(2)(i)(A)&(B) (West); 45 C.F.R. § 164.504(e)(ii)(A)&(B).

- at contract termination, return or destroy all PHI received from, or created or received on behalf of, the covered entity or, if not feasible, to continue the contractual safeguards for such PHI.[13]

Financial institutions are required under the Gramm-Leach-Bliley Act to address protection of customer information in the custody of their service providers. Thus, entities subject to the FTC's Standards for Safeguarding Customer Information[14] must, as part of their comprehensive information security program, oversee service providers that receive, maintain, process, or otherwise are permitted access to customer information as they provide services to such entities.[15] Specifically, such entities must take reasonable steps to select and retain service providers capable of maintaining appropriate safeguards for customer information, and must also require such service providers by contract to implement and maintain appropriate safeguards.[16]

Entities subject to the FTC's Red Flags Rule, when administering their required Identity Theft Prevention Program, must exercise appropriate and effective oversight of service provider arrangements,[17] such as by conducting due diligence when selecting service providers and contractually requiring data security safeguards. The FTC's Disposal Rule requires covered persons to properly dispose of consumer information to protect against unauthorized access to or use of such information in connection with its disposal.[18] One compliance option is conducting due diligence and then contracting with and monitoring contract compliance of a records destruction business to compliantly dispose of material containing consumer information.[19] Such due diligence may include: reviewing an independent audit of the disposal company's operations or Disposal Rule compliance, obtaining information from several references or other reliable sources, requiring certification of the disposal company by a recognized trade association or similar third party,

[12] 45 C.F.R. § 164.314(a)(2)(i)(C); 45 C.F.R. § 164.504(e)(ii)(C).
[13] 45 C.F.R. § 164.504(e)(ii)(J).
[14] 16 C.F.R. § 314 (West).
[15] 16 C.F.R. § 314.2(d) (West); 16 C.F.R. § 314.4(d).
[16] 16 C.F.R. § 314.4(d)(1)&(2).
[17] 16 C.F.R. § 681.1(e)(4) (West).
[18] 16 C.F.R. § 682.3(a) (West 2005).
[19] 16 C.F.R. § 682.3(b)(3).

reviewing and evaluating the disposal company's information security policies or procedures, or taking other appropriate measures to determine the disposal company's competency and integrity.[20]

California, Maryland, Nevada, and Rhode Island mandate that businesses that disclose state residents' PII to non-affiliated third parties must, by contract, require that the third party establish reasonable security procedures and practices to protect the PII from unauthorized access, destruction, use, modification, or disclosure.[21]

Various states require persons and businesses that possess protected personal information of state residents to maintain reasonable security procedures and practices to protect such PII from unauthorized use or disclosure, and service provider possession of PII should therefore be addressed.[22] The Massachusetts law mandating that entities that own or possess PII of Commonwealth residents must maintain a written comprehensive information security program further requires that the program include oversight of service providers, by taking reasonable steps in selecting and retaining service providers capable of maintaining appropriate and compliant security measures, and by requiring such service providers by contract to compliantly protect such PII.[23] Under Oregon law, the information security program is deemed compliant if it includes specified safeguards such as, among other matters, selecting service providers capable of maintaining appropriate safeguards, and requiring those safeguards by contract.[24] Alaska, Hawaii, Illinois, North Carolina, and South Carolina have similar legal requirements regarding third-party records disposal arrangements.[25]

---

[20] *Id.*

[21] Ann. Cal. Civ. Code § 1798.81.5(b) (West 2006); Md. Code Ann., Com. Law § 14-3503(b) (West 2008); Nev. Rev. Stat. § 603A.210(2) (2006); *and* R.I. Gen. Laws § 11-49.2-2(3) (West).

[22] Ark. Code Ann. § 4-110-104(b) (2005); Cal. Civ. Code § 1798.81.5(b) (2006); Md. Code Ann., Com. Law § 14-3503(a) (West); Nev. Rev. Stat. § 603A.210(1); O.R. Rev. Stat. § 646A.622(1) (West); R.I. Gen. Laws § 11-49.2-2(2) (West); Tex. Bus. & Com. Code Ann. § 501.052(a) (2009); Utah Code Ann. § 13-44-201(1) (West).

[23] 201 Mass. Code Regs. 17.03(2)(f) (West).

[24] O.R. Rev. Stat. Ann. § 646A.622(2)(d)(A)(v).

[25] Alaska Stat. Ann. § 45.48.510-20 (West); Haw. Rev. Stat. Ann. § 487R-2(c) (West); 815 Ill. Comp. Stat. 530/40(c) (West); N.C. Gen. Stat. Ann. § 75-64(c) (West); S.C. Code Ann. § 37-20-190(A)-(B) (2008).

Thus, most companies that allow third parties to store or process protected information on the company's behalf must comply with data security laws explicitly requiring service provider contracts with data security provisions and an appropriate level of due diligence in selecting such service providers. Even if no such requirements directly apply, companies still face the risk of significant exposure to hard costs and reputational damage resulting from service provider security breaches that trigger data breach notification laws.

If the company pursues privacy and data security compliance in an isolated, autonomous manner, it will likely ensure that its service provider contracts contain the required language regarding the service provider's obligations for the security of protected information. The company may also perform due diligence in its vendor selection process regarding the potential service provider's capabilities for and attention to data security, and may even periodically monitor or assess the data security programs of its service providers. These steps of course do help in compliance with the strict letter of privacy and data security laws. Nevertheless, such companies will still face risks and exposures for data security breaches and also for breach response.

In contrast, companies that adopt the information governance approach understand that their use of service providers to store or process information (including protected information) is a focal point of information-related compliance requirements and risks, including but by no means limited to, privacy and data security. Such companies will assess their overall use of service providers by considering information-related compliance requirements and risks from multiple perspectives, including the disciplines of privacy and data security, records and information management, and litigation. These companies will then put in place the structures, policies and processes, resources, and accountability to provide reasonable assurance of compliance with applicable requirements and control of identified risks.

Let us consider the hypothetical company ORG Inc., which has adopted the information governance approach. ORG has protected information subject to privacy and data security requirements, which it regularly transfers to the custody of various service providers in the ordinary operation of its business, for storage, such as through cloud computing and off-site paper records management, and also for information processing.

From the isolated perspective of privacy and data security compliance, ORG appears to satisfy the explicit requirements of applicable privacy and data security laws. Among other matters, ORG conducts due diligence on data security capabilities when selecting and retaining service providers, and it contractually requires its service providers to have safeguards in place to ensure security for such protected information. ORG also periodically reviews the contractual performance of its service providers, including their data security for protected information.

But through an information governance assessment, ORG determines that its internal requirements for records retention periods are not being consistently followed by its various service providers, such that some service providers may be retaining ORG's information for either a shorter or longer period of time than is required under the ORG records retention schedule. ORG also concludes that its legal hold process may not have consistently included consideration of information relevant to past litigation that was in the possession of its various service providers, yet arguably within the "control" of ORG for discovery purposes.

ORG now, based on its assessment, adjusts its approach to governing information stored or processed by its service providers. First, ORG will use a classification structure to help it identify what information is in the custody of its various service providers. ORG may use a traditional records retention schedule that establishes its retention periods for such information, and it may also use an information security matrix to confirm the safeguards applicable to such information. Alternatively, ORG may establish an Information Governance Matrix, which categorizes all of ORG's information types and indicates both the applicable records retention period and also the applicable security controls. ORG may refer to its mapping of existing legal holds to determine what customer information in the possession of service providers should be preserved. ORG might also, by itself or through a requirement imposed upon its service providers, track specifically what items of information are held by its individual service providers. This tracking of protected information has the privacy and data security benefit of facilitating response actions in the event of a breach. It also helps make records retention period compliance actionable, as well as make execution of legal holds more efficient and accurate.

Second, ORG will focus on its service provider contracts and its internal policies and processes. ORG will ensure that its contracts with service providers contain terms requiring the service providers to comply not only with data security safeguards for protected information, but also with ORG's retention periods for the information, as well as protocols for responsive compliance with ORG's legal holds. ORG will also provide direction to its internal procurement and contract management functions so that information governance controls beyond data security safeguards are imbedded in the processes for selecting and retaining service providers, for negotiating service contracts, and for managing such contracts.

Third, ORG will provide the necessary resources to accomplish the steps listed above, which end up being minimal. ORG will simply supplement its existing processes already in place for privacy and data security oversight of service providers, so that they also encompass compliance with records retention periods and legal holds as applicable. Essentially the same internal ORG business functions are involved as before, with processes and procedures adjusted to address the broader range of information-related issues.

Last, ORG will ensure accountability for its adjusted approach to governing information held by its service providers. ORG will add records retention and legal hold compliance to its existing reviews of service providers for data security compliance. It will also modify its internal audit checklists for its internal procurement and contract management functions to determine whether its information governance protocols are being followed.

As a result of these actions, ORG will better ensure its compliance with information governance legal requirements applicable to it and its service providers, including privacy and data security, records retention and lifecycle management, and litigation preservation and discovery. ORG will also better control its information-related risks in these areas. This improvement includes better control of risks and exposures for data security breaches, by gaining a more specific understanding of what protected information is held by such service providers, by establishing the means of more efficient and timely breach response, and by limiting the unnecessary and uncontrolled retention by service providers of ORG's protected information.

The more thorough service provider contract and review approach adopted by ORG will also send the clear message to such service providers that information governance is a high priority for doing business with ORG. And ultimately, ORG's management will have reasonable assurance that information-related risks involving service providers, including privacy and data security, are being adequately controlled.

Conclusion

Information governance, as an integrated approach to achieving information compliance and risk control, is an ideal strategy for enhancing a company's privacy and data security safeguards. It is also a more mature, coherent strategy than the traditional approach, in which companies' various information-related disciplines operate autonomously.

If the approach described above seems impractical or onerous, one is reminded of former US Deputy Attorney General Paul McNulty, who famously remarked, "The cost of non-compliance is great. If you think compliance is expensive, try non-compliance."[26] Indeed, the information governance approach, if properly pursued, results in overall savings for the company, by avoiding unnecessary information-related expenses and reducing the likelihood of costly information-related exposures.

Most importantly, the information governance approach strengthens a company's ability to meet information compliance requirements and control information-related risks. In today's complex information environment, that is especially the case for privacy and data security.

Key Takeaways

- Companies must adapt to the challenge of information flowing freely in and out of their traditional perimeters, finding new strategies to apply existing compliance requirements to a complex, rapidly evolving information environment.

---

[26] *See* Doug Cornelius, *McNulty Keynote on a Tale of Two Sectors*, COMPLIANCE BUILDING, http://www.compliancebuilding.com/2009/06/04/mcnulty-keynote-on-a-tale-of-two-sectors/.

- At any given moment, the same information may be covered by privacy and data security requirements, be subject to records retention and information management requirements, and be under a preservation duty in pending or impending litigation. In light of the attendant risks and costs, such an environment demands a strategic, systematic response from the company.
- Companies pursuing an information governance approach integrate their thinking and actions regarding information across the traditional information-related disciplines of privacy and data security, records and information management, and litigation preservation and collection. Such organizations first seek to understand the full range of compliance requirements and risks concerning their information arising out of these disciplines. They then establish information policies and controls that efficiently and effectively address information compliance and risk in a holistic way.
- By adopting an information governance approach, companies reap the additional benefit of stronger compliance and risk control for privacy and data security.

Peter Sloan is a Husch Blackwell LLP partner and founding member of the firm's Information Governance Group. For over a decade, Mr. Sloan has focused his practice on how companies can best manage their records and information. Mr. Sloan helps companies across the country create, validate, and update records retention schedules; implement information compliance systems; develop legal hold processes and strategies; and deploy risk management approaches to e-mail and other digital information. At his direction, the firm has categorized over 56,000 records retention legal requirements and legal considerations found in the statutes and regulations of the United States federal system and the fifty states. Mr. Sloan has presented at seminars and conferences throughout the United States on records retention, legal hold preservation, and information governance. Mr. Sloan is a member of ARMA International, AIIM, and The Sedona Conference® Working Group 1 on Electronic Document Retention and Production.

Autonomy: The Key Theory for Understanding the Evolution of US Privacy Law

Edward R. McNicholas

Partner

Sidley Austin LLP

ASPATORE

Introduction

United States privacy law is in a troublesome mess. The law could be reassuring consumers, convincing the world that the United States remains a beacon of liberty, and protecting the foundations of our freedoms. But it is instead, to some degree, failing in each of these tasks, and leaving many with little sense of the course of the law's development in this area.

There are many causes of this incoherence, but a key problem is our disagreement about the purpose of privacy protections. In the United States, many have addressed privacy as merely a formalistic, contractual matter requiring a posted privacy policy, but significant pressures are calling into question this model of "notice and choice." Other models have focused on the elimination of privacy harms in the *use*, as opposed to the *collection*, of personal data. However many criticize this theory's failure to appreciate the potential rights of the data subject to avoid an unwanted electronic gaze. Others have seen privacy law as the primary means to protect privacy as one in a litany of "fundamental" human rights. This perspective is often criticized as failing to balance perceived competing rights, including rights of commerce and expression.

Still others have pressed for agreement on certain "fair information principles" that demonstrate a commitment to certain ideals that is shared across jurisdictions, such as requirements that data subjects receive notice and choice. An approach based on fair information principles can indeed be useful in seeking agreement on substantive commitments to particular legal restrictions even in the absence of a shared theory of the importance of such commitments. This approach does offer some significant possibilities of building a bridge across vastly different social meanings and legal systems for privacy in various different countries across the Asia Pacific region, Europe, and the Americas. This approach, however, seeks to build a practical consensus, not a shared theory of the privacy, and so it lacks significant power to explain the evolution of privacy in any given culture. For instance, fair information principles may include the idea that notice must be given, but it will not illuminate what areas are likely to be deemed to require "special" notice in any given culture. Thus, for all of its practical and diplomatic utility, a fair information principle will not provide us with a theory of privacy that will help us to predict its further evolution.

This lack of consensus for privacy has not only affected its theory, but it has also obscured some of the fundamental transformations taking place with respect to our relationship with technology. While I no doubt fail to appreciate the scope of some of these changes, it does seem clear to me that explicating the transformation of privacy should illuminate some of the deeper currents that are driving the long-term development of US privacy law.

Foundations of the Concept of Privacy

Understanding this fundamental shift requires us to return to the foundations of privacy. Warren and Brandeis famously celebrated "the right to be let alone," but the right they explained was a right against "the evil of invasion of privacy by the newspapers" designed to be "the right to protect one's self from pen portraiture, from a discussion by the press of one's private affairs."[1]

US privacy law has continued to find certain areas of life worthy of seclusion. Posted mail, voice communications, medical records, financial records, and a few other areas have been protected by sector-specific statutory protections. These protections, however, have been trimmed—sometimes materially—by the so-called "third party" doctrine,[2] which denies any *constitutional* protection to data held by third parties. These areas are protected only by those limited statutory protections that Congress chooses to afford, and subject to the *constitutional* protections of the freedom of speech afforded corporate entities that may hold these records.

---

[1] Samuel D. Warren & Louis D. Brandeis, *The Right to Privacy*, 4 HARV. L. REV. 193, 219 (1890)

[2] In the seminal case of *United States* v. *Miller*, 425 U.S. 435 (1976), the United States Supreme Court opined that it has held repeatedly that the Fourth Amendment does not prohibit the obtaining of information revealed to a third party and conveyed by him to government authorities, even if the information is revealed on the assumption that it will be used only for a limited purpose and the confidence placed in the third party will not be betrayed. Accordingly, the Supreme Court found that there is no constitutional privacy interest in bank records held by banks. Three years later, the United States Supreme Court again emphasized that it "consistently has held that a person has no legitimate expectation of privacy in information he voluntarily turns over to third parties." *Smith v. Maryland*, 442 U.S. 735, 743-44 (1979) (internal citations omitted).

Although the current model of US privacy law has its virtues, the slow statutory accretion of specific restrictions has not shown a beacon of freedom to the world, as one would have hoped. In the meantime, more countries are choosing to follow a more comprehensive, European Union-modeled approach to privacy, which deems it a fundamental human right.[3] Starting from Germany and spreading across Europe and now into the Americas, Asia, and Africa, this more comprehensive, fundamental approach to privacy has resulted in the widespread adoption of omnibus fair information principles as a means of vindicating privacy interests.[4] In large part, these norms have reflected a response to the cultural history of World War II, the development of a more unified Europe, and a desire to preserve these cultural values in ever globalizing markets.

To be sure, portions of the US privacy regime do reflect similar fair information principles. The United States' own Federal Trade Commission (FTC) has indeed championed its version of such fair information principles, urging thoughtful consideration of privacy issues (often referred to as "privacy by design"), affording consumers simplified choices, and urging greater transparency. The FTC has advanced the notion that providing consumers with notice and choice about some of the uses of their personal information serves some meaningful purpose of expressing respect for the individual. The limitations of this agency, however, have hampered its recognition as a defender of privacy, and have inhibited its ability to challenge Internet economic models in which data profiles about consumers are the product. The agency's approach has thus rarely outright forbidden the collection of personal information, and it has an overarching focus on data subjects who are consumers, thus not explicitly covering privacy rights of employees or more broadly, of citizens. The FTC has generated this law only by grafting its institutional designs onto statutory authority meant to prohibit unfair and deceptive acts and practices, not expressly designed to protect privacy per se. This ambiguous statutory mandate has undercut the FTC's ability to advance US privacy law.

---

[3] Directive 95/46/EC of the European Parliament and of the Council of 24 October 1995 on the protection of individuals with regard to the processing of personal data on the free movement of such data, OJ L281/31, 23.11.1995.

[4] The term "fair information principles" appears to stem from a 1973 report of Department of Health, Education, and Welfare (HEW), which recommended a "Code of Fair Information Practices," although a German Lander already had a similar privacy law in place prior to the HEW report.

The deeper issue—shared both in Europe and in the United States—is that these often more formalistic notions of privacy lead to a paradigm in which privacy notices and check boxes can be seen as surrogates for the protection of some vague notion of "privacy" without much overt consideration of the goals that privacy serves. Too often, corporate and governmental privacy programs are seen to involve little more than posting external privacy policies. This notice-and-choice paradigm is widely seen as having failed to provide substantial protection for consumers and citizens, in large part because its relies on a contractual ideal of a deal struck by equally informed and equally powerful beings, a construct which finds little empirical support in the world of the Internet and our modern republic.

The exponential growth of big data, however, is rapidly unmasking such superficial Potemkin privacy. Every day floods of data pour from our smartphones, houses, and cars, revealing our musings, locations, social connections, vices, and virtues. Cameras—soon to recognize us—monitor our movements inside offices and stores and on the streets. Wireless broadband network connectivity is becoming ubiquitous in urban areas, and the popularization of computationally intensive algorithmic tools that deliver insights from large data sets (Big Data) is sparking new interest in the promise of computing to address a host of social needs from food distribution to the spread of disease. Soon the Internet of Things will be more apparent as devices from road sensors, to cameras, to RFID chips in everything from clothing to lawnmowers, are able to collect information about the daily lives of their owners. As these sensors begin to speak to each other, they will share more and more information. The Internet of Things will indeed involve a deluge of sensors so that our very physical environment will interact with itself and generate a comprehensive data portrait of our lives. This portrait may well be robust enough to predict to some significant degree of certainty our future behaviors and opinions based on the broad data sets of our past.

The coming Internet of Things will thus very likely serve to pressure, if not overwhelm, the current notice-and-choice paradigm. It was at best questionable to suppose that consumers read and understand lengthy privacy notices drafted in robust legalese on the back pages of websites. However, now many of the devices that will accumulate, share, and use data about us will lack even any sort of consumer interface—much less a screen on which a policy could be displayed. As automatic data collection moves to the physical world, we face the issue of how can a toaster, a microwave, or a facial recognition camera you pass on the way to your morning coffee provide you with such notice? Detailed notices posted on websites may continue to assist companies in expressing their privacy norms—and regulators in judging compliance with those norms. Such notices, however, will likely play little role in providing consumers with the sort of ubiquitous customized services and data that are desired—or note—by the consumers themselves—but not necessarily by the regulators and self-styled privacy advocates with the inclination to assess such privacy documentation. Indeed, these "privacy policy" forms could well increasingly make clear that little "privacy" exists. If mere awareness of inundation of surveillance is the purpose of privacy, then perhaps Scott McNealy's famous line "You have zero privacy anyway…Get over it"[5] is correct.

Privacy Means and Ends

My thought here rests fundamentally on a rejection of Mr. McNealy's epigram. A legal regime that merely informs the public that it has no privacy is not worth protecting, and it will certainly not gather sufficient popular and political support. However privacy, particularly in the United States, is more than awareness of surveillance; it is and has been the "right to be let alone." That right enjoys wide support across the political spectrum, in part because this right stands not merely on its own, but rather serves the ends of protecting individual autonomy, that is, the person's ability to govern his or her own growth and flourishing.

The current focus of privacy protections is on providing safeguards for any and all data concerning an individual. This approach to privacy, however, has wrapped in on itself and forced us to protect our Internet searches for recipes and cycling shorts with the same degree of protection afforded Internet searches for religious readings, political inspiration, and familial connections. This lack of focus or substantive differentiation misses the point entirely that privacy is known and experienced as a second-order good, useful only to the extent that it protects more fundamental liberties.

[5] Stephen Manes, *Private Lives? Not Ours!*, PC WORLD (April 18, 2000).

Who truly cares about all of the data that may possibly refer to them? The size of my shoe, the fact that I like green more than blue, my choice of cars: do any these facts merit anyone's interest, much less protection? Salesmen may of course find this interesting, but why should we as a society commit the resources of the state to attacking the engines of commerce? Surely the European notion of sensitive personal data or the sectoral approach of the United States have some merit in proclaiming that some areas of life are different than others. However neither the United States nor the European approach has successfully articulated a consistent theory of their limitations and role. Such a theory could point us—and indeed guide us—toward a more coherent future for privacy, and provide some ability to chart the future course of US privacy law.

Privacy and Autonomy

Describing such a theory is certainly beyond the ken of such a short essay, but we can point to such a theory that explains the future evolution of privacy by looking back briefly to the prior meaning of privacy starting with Brandeis and focusing on the evolution of those interests seen in constitutionally protected personal and family sexual and reproductive rights.[6] To some, rights to abortion or LGBT equality have no connection to privacy in the sense that we are discussing. Rarely would one find an FTC official citing this robust body of case law in defense of US privacy law. However it is important to recognize that *Roe* expressly adopted the mantle of privacy as it relates to intimate personal decisions, stating that "right of privacy, whether it be founded in the Fourteenth Amendment's concept of personal liberty and restrictions upon state action, as we feel it is, or, as the district court determined, in the Ninth Amendment's reservation of rights to the people, is broad enough to encompass a woman's decision whether or not to terminate her pregnancy." *Roe*'s right to privacy indeed stemmed from the "right to marital privacy" recognized in *Griswold v. Connecticut* (allowing use of contraceptives).[7] *Griswold* itself built upon the rights recognized in *Meyer v. Nebraska*,[8] "to marry, establish a home, and bring up children," and *Pierce v. Society of Sisters*,[9] in which the

[6] *Roe v. Wade*, 410 U.S. 113, 122 (1973).
[7] *Griswold v. Connecticut*, 381 U.S. 479 (1965).
[8] *Meyer v. Nebraska*, 262 U.S. 390, 399 (1923).
[9] *Pierce v. Soc'y of the Sisters of the Holy Names of Jesus & Mary*, 268 U.S. 510 (1925).

Supreme Court invoked privacy as the reason to allow Catholic parents to send their children to Catholic schools, striking down an Oregon Act requiring public school because it "unreasonably interferes with the liberty of parents and guardians to direct the upbringing and education of children under their control." 268 U.S. at 268 U.S. 534-535. All of these cases defended "the private realm of family life which the state cannot enter."[10] Indeed, Justice Kennedy built on the long-standing pillar of privacy when, in *Lawrence v. Texas*, he struck down a Texas sodomy statute because of "its intrusion into the personal and private life of the individual."[11] This evolution was built upon the recognition that certain spheres of life are more central to the ability to govern your own life.

Although some may suggest that these protections are a hodge-podge of invented entitlements, each of the privacy rights are expressions of the fundamental good which privacy serves: the right to personal autonomy; that is, the ability to enjoy a sphere in which certain matters are beyond the question of the state. Privacy fits well within this sphere, next to freedoms of speech, religion, and association as bulwarks that support human flourishing. As Peggy Noonan recently observed, "Privacy is connected to personhood. It has to do with intimate things—the innards of your head and heart, the workings of your mind—and the boundary between those things and the world outside."[12] Privacy in this sense penetrates far more deeply into the US legal system than insistence of providing notices of privacy practices and superficial choices about the uses of data.

This sense of privacy as autonomy likewise maps well onto the Fourth Amendment's bulwark against "unreasonable searches and seizures,"[13] based on the fundamental premise that a search is constitutional if it does not violate a person's "reasonable" or "legitimate" expectation of privacy.[14] Across the political spectrum, notions of privacy have continually been most respected in those areas most closely associated with family and personal life, or as Justice Scalia recently opined:

---

[10] *Prince v. Massachusetts*, 321 U. S. 158, 166 (1944).

[11] *Lawrence v. Texas*, 539 U.S. 558 (2003).

[12] Peggy Noonan, *What We Lose if We Give Up Privacy: A civil libertarian reflects on the dangers of the surveillance state*, WALL ST. J., Aug. 16, 2013.

[13] U.S. CONST. amend. IV.

[14] *Katz* v. *United States*, 389 U.S. 347, 362 (1967) (Harlan, J., concurring) (recognizing a reasonable expectation of privacy in the substantive content of telephone discussions).

> We...regard the area "immediately surrounding and associated with the home"—what our cases call the curtilage—as "part of the home itself for Fourth Amendment purposes." ...That principle has ancient and durable roots. Just as the distinction between the home and the open fields is "as old as the common law," ...so too is the identity of home and what Blackstone called the "curtilage or homestall," for the "house protects and privileges all its branches and appurtenants." ...This area around the home is "intimately linked to the home, both physically and psychologically," and is where "privacy expectations are most heightened."[15]

The protection of the constitutional amendments of course do not apply to most private conduct directly,[16] but they do provide a compelling frame for understanding appropriate spheres for privacy protections. It is no accident that the Fourth Amendment focuses on inquiry into people's "persons, houses, papers, and effects," and no surprise that privacy protections for the home and family have fit most comfortably into US privacy law.[17] Likewise, the Fifth Amendment protections against self-incrimination serve to recognize and protect a zone of intellectual autonomy about one's personal motivations and papers.

The four distinct, widely recognized privacy torts likewise support the autonomy interests at stake during an invasion of privacy: (1) intrusion upon the plaintiff's seclusion or solitude, or into the plaintiff's private affairs; (2) appropriation, for the defendant's advantage, of the plaintiff's name or likeness; (3) public disclosure of private facts about the plaintiff; and (4) publicity that places the plaintiff in a false light in the public eye.[18] Indeed, the core privacy tort of intrusion upon seclusion fundamentally depends upon the idea that the breach of seclusion is itself actionable, and

---

[15] *Florida v. Jardines*, 133 S. Ct. 1409 (2013) (citing *inter alia* 4 W. Blackstone, COMMENTARIES ON THE LAWS OF ENGLAND 223, 225 (1769)).

[16] Significantly, the Fourth Amendment itself "is wholly inapplicable to a search or seizure, even an unreasonable one, effected by a private individual not acting as an agent of the Government or with the participation or knowledge of any governmental official." *United States v. Jacobsen*, 466 U.S. 109, 113 (1984) (internal quotation omitted).

[17] U.S. CONST. amend. IV.

[18] *See* RESTATEMENT (SECOND) OF TORTS §§ 652A-E (1977).

hence the common law recognizes the protection of the very basic form of privacy present in seclusion outside of the constitutional context.

Consistently, however, the international dialogue about fair information practices has neglected these core constitutional and common law groundings and instead rested on more administrative notions of fair information principles, which are at least not overtly connected to the dignitary norms of our constitutional system. Subjugating long-standing constitutional and common-law-based rationale for privacy protections has lead us into the current, un-compelling debate over notice-and-choice privacy protection. It has blinded observers from the deeper currents of US privacy law that will drive the next generation of responses to technological progress.

Conceptualizing privacy as protecting autonomy has far more explanatory power in considering the future of privacy than worrying whether a toaster can display a privacy policy. Far more significantly, privacy as autonomy can function better to define the borders of the state, and protect the border of the self within our society. Although these borders allow for isolation—the right to be let alone—it is important to emphasize that these borders have never been sought for the sole purpose of isolation. The privacy borders of the rights of autonomy allow for the possibility of self-definition that is antecedent to and the product of intimacy and sharing. The protection of individual privacy can accordingly serve the goal of human connectedness and social sharing without losing its core.

Implications of Privacy as Autonomy

Conceiving of privacy as a tool designed to protect the autonomy of individuals—primarily as citizens, and secondarily as consumers and employees—echoes this actual development of privacy laws. If this theory maps onto what may be recognized as a shared purpose of privacy law, it will point to the evolution of privacy laws along several interesting avenues, and it will serve to align the future of privacy with protections that even Mr. McNealy would likely recognize as worth maintaining. Three key points flow from this re-conceptualization of the importance of privacy.

First, most fundamentally, this notion of privacy as autonomy functions significantly as a bulwark against the excessive and unwanted incursions of state power. It suggests that our continual focus on the Fourth Amendment's and Ninth Amendment's restrictions on governmental intrusions will remain a central feature of US privacy law, in sharp contrast to limited European notions of privacy that seem to focus on private corporate intrusions and indeed exclude matters of national defense and state security from the directive altogether.[19]

Second, the notion of privacy as autonomy suggests that the government's effort to regulate private corporate information should be limited by the usefulness of those efforts in the service of protecting individual autonomy. Private corporations certainly have the capacity to oppress human flourishing—in many instances almost as much as any government authority. One can certainly recall that the long history of company towns and exposure of workers to obscene working conditions that marked periods of our development fueled in part by a belief in a contractual paradigm most fully articulated in *Lochner v. New York*.[20]

Recognizing some governmental role in the protection of individuals, however, does not suggest that our privacy is best protected by a general regulation of information within corporations. As *Sorrell v. IMS Health Inc.*, teaches, government cannot punish speech because of its commercial motivation, and the role of free market as a counter-weight to the strength of the state cannot be dismissed.[21] Such considerations should significantly dampen any move toward an EU-style omnibus regulation of commercial activity, or at least they should serve to limit the authority of the government to function as a guardian of data in the hands of persons and

---

[19] Directive 95/46/EC of the European Parliament and of the Council of 24 October 1995 on the protection of individuals with regard to the processing of personal data on the free movement of such data, OJ L281/31, 23.11.1995. ("(13) Whereas the activities referred to in Titles V and VI of the Treaty on European Union regarding public safety, defence, State security or the activities of the State in the area of criminal laws fall outside the scope of Community law…(16) Whereas the processing of sound and image data, such as in cases of video surveillance, does not come within the scope of this Directive if it is carried out for the purposes of public security, defence, national security or in the course of State activities relating to the area of criminal law or of other activities which do not come within the scope of Community law").

[20] *Lochner v. New York*, 198 U.S. 45 (1905).

[21] *Sorrell v. IMS Health Inc.*, 131 S. Ct. 2653 (2011).

corporations. In any case, the omnibus protection of privacy in commercial activity is *not necessary* to the protection of privacy as autonomy. Indeed, to the extent that commercial activity is exalted as the core of human expression, the protection of privacy in commercial activity could be an impediment to happiness.

My idea is that the US legal system—both common law and statutory—will evolve to protect an Internet in which individuals have highly reticulated controls about their social interactions built into experiences. Controls that respect and empower autonomous choice and customization of experience can flourish without indulging a formalistic *Lochnerian* fiction of contract. These controls should allow *individuals* the choice to share information within close circles of friends or with broader groupings or everyone, based on their decisions. This empowerment of the individuals to connect as they desire should be a fundamental goal and driver of privacy law based on the course of its development to date. And it is crucial that the law develop rapidly to preserve this autonomy, lest the potential legal norms in this area become overwhelmed by Mr. McNealy's technological determinism.

The third key insight is that an appropriate focus should be on the development of a governmental role supporting the protection of the autonomy of the individual. Restrictions against surveillance so pervasive as to leave no sense of useful isolation will be important, as well as the development of contextually appropriate spheres of information sharing. The important project for the government will thus be to ensure special recognition in the privacy dialogue for matters of religion, association, health, sexuality, family life, and speech. The preservation of human autonomy, however, is not well defended by check boxes and privacy notices. Rather, substantive limits on the collection, uses, and sharing of certain particularly sensitive information should remain a useful tool to ensure the protection of the realm of those areas most connected to personal life.

Conclusion: Tracking Privacy into Policy

Retracing privacy to its roots gives us a powerful tool to project a possible long-term path for the evolution of US privacy law across several key areas of growth including cloud computing, mobile computing, social media, big data, and the Internet of Things.

In the context of cloud computing, there is currently an intense debate surrounding European regulators' desire to impose a mechanism for the extraterritorial vindication of privacy rights for EU citizens outside of the European Economic Area. Fundamentally, the EU has pushed this approach based on the perceived superiority of its approach, and its desire to protect human rights.[22] However, appreciating US privacy law as fundamentally driven by the protection of autonomy may give the United States a counter-weight to the human rights language invoked by the European Union. Efforts to patch together a coherent theory from a cluster of sectoral laws have not proved persuasive. This debate, however, will remain a defining struggle over the sort of protections afforded to individuals.

Mobile computing and social media will likewise remain flash points given the potential for the pervasive collection of information about individuals, and the "Big Data" analysis of the social graph, communications, and movements of individuals. The need to focus US privacy laws on the protection of autonomy is essential to ensure the pervasive adoption of these technologies. Moreover, the consistent recognition of the primacy of respect for individual autonomy should help to deter unduly restrictive luddites bent on deterring technology out of ignorance without capitulating to a *1984* surveillance state. The coming Internet of Things will escalate the collection of data about individuals to unprecedented heights, and it will do so in non-intuitive ways well beyond the ability of the notice-and-choice paradigm to adsorb.

---

[22] The current approach of the European Union to the proposed Data Protection Regulation entirely neglects its expansive extraterritorial effects. European jurisdiction over companies that lack a physical presence in the European Union should, in theory, be exercised only sparingly and in a manner consistent with the complex considerations of international comity. Under certain circumstances, companies lacking an EU presence should be subject to EU regulation, but the legal analysis here should be a multi-factored consideration of the interests of both legal systems. The United States long recognized the demands of comity in suits involving foreign states, either as parties or as sovereigns with a coordinate interest in the litigation. *See Hilton v. Guyot*, 159 U.S. 113 (1895). The Supreme Court in *Societe Nationale Industrielle Aerospatiale v. U.S. Dist. Court for S. Dist. of Iowa*, 482 U.S. 522, 544 (1987) and in other cases has indeed required United States regulatory agencies to consider international comity interests.

We stand today at the threshold of a fundamental shift in privacy. We can see an opportunity to refocus privacy protections on individual autonomy. This advancement of US privacy law can and should serve to reassure US consumers, convince the world that the United States remains a beacon of liberty, and protect the foundations of our freedom.

Key Takeaways

- Lack of consensus for the purpose of privacy has affected its theory and obscured some of the fundamental transformations taking place with respect to our relationship with technology.
- Too often, corporate and governmental privacy programs are seen to involve little more than posting external privacy policies. This notice-and-choice paradigm is widely seen as having failed to provide substantial protection for consumers and citizens, leading a technological determinism that privacy is an antiquated and moribund idea.
- Privacy as autonomy can function better to define the borders of the state, and protect the border of the self within our society.
- The US legal system—both common law and statutory—will evolve to protect an Internet in which individuals have highly reticulated controls about their social interactions built into experiences. Fundamentally, US consumers will demand a privacy regime in which their autonomy is respected, and they will not long support a regime driven by formulaic and unread legal notices.

Edward R. McNicholas is a partner in the Washington, DC office of the international law firm Sidley Austin LLP and a global coordinator of its Privacy, Data Security, and Information Law practice. Mr. McNicholas's practice focuses on clients facing complex information technology, constitutional, and privacy issues in civil and white-collar criminal matters. Mr. McNicholas concentrates his practice on trial and appellate representations of technologically sophisticated clients including telecommunications carriers, electronic service providers, financial services companies, pharmaceutical manufacturers, and other companies facing complex personal information issues.

Mr. McNicholas has significant experience with a wide-range of cutting-edge Internet and information law matters involving privacy and data protection, electronic surveillance, information security, cloud computing, trade secrets, social media, locational privacy, e-commerce, and national security. Mr. McNicholas and Sidley's Privacy and Data Security practice were selected for CHAMBERS USA: AMERICA'S LEADING LAWYERS FOR BUSINESS *for 2008-2013 as well as* CHAMBERS GLOBAL *for 2010-2013, the 2011-2013* LEGAL 500, *and* THE INTERNATIONAL WHO'S WHO OF INTERNET, E-COMMERCE & DATA PROTECTION LAWYERS *2011-2013. Chambers USA (2013) notes that Mr. McNicholas "wins praise for his 'depth of experience and ability to bring technology issues together to provide information we can act on.'" Mr. McNicholas previously served as an Associate Counsel to President Clinton. In that capacity, he advised senior White House staff regarding various Independent Counsel, congressional and grand jury investigations. Mr. McNicholas is a graduate of the Harvard Law School, where he served as an editor of the* HARVARD LAW REVIEW, *and Princeton University, where he studied public policy at the Woodrow Wilson School for Public and International Affairs.*

Acknowledgment: *The author wishes to acknowledge the review and comments of Colleen Brown and Vivek Mohan, associates at Sidley Austin LLP. The views expressed in this article do not constitute legal advice and are those of the author alone and do not necessarily reflect those of his partners, firm, or clients.*

Accountable Care Organizations and the Downside to Coordination: Increased Opportunity for Data Breach

Mark Mattioli

Chair, Health Law and Governmental Compliance Groups

Marshall Dennehey Warner Coleman and Goggin

ASPATORE

Introduction

Delivery of healthcare is changing from a single provider culture to an integrated approach. Much of this push has come about as a result of healthcare reform efforts that incentivized the use of the Accountable Care Organization (ACO) through the Medicare Shared Savings Program. Under an ACO, each provider is "accountable" for the totality of the care provided to the patient. This is believed to meet the triple aim of reducing cost, improving care to the individual, and improving care to the population. ACOs that save money are entitled to a share of the savings.

For the program to work, it is vital that components of the healthcare system share data among themselves. Without a robust electronic health record, the goals of the ACO cannot be achieved. With this sharing of information comes additional risks to all parties involved in the ACO. This chapter explores some of those risks so that they can be understood and managed.

Overview: Unprecedented Cooperation

The delivery of healthcare services is facing a paradigm shift from independent practitioners performing services in a silo to an interactive and coordinated approach where each provider is viewed simply as part of the overall patient care. Information and data sharing is the glue that binds these divergent practices together. In theory, information flows in real time over an unimpeded pipeline. A laboratory test given to a patient is transmitted instantly to the patient's primary care physician, specialists, and the hospital where their patient is about to undergo a medical procedure. This interactive way of treating patients is hoped to result in higher quality care and reduced costs because expensive complications and hospitalizations can be avoided. This is the central thrust of the Accountable Care Organization (ACO).

While the theory behind such organizations is not all that new, the push to form ACOs was given a boost by the Affordable Care Act, as part of health care reform. To date, the Centers for Medicare and Medicaid Services (CMS) has certified 220 organizations to participate in the Medicare Shared Savings Program (MSSP), under which providers can be rewarded by receiving a percentage of the money they save the government for providing services to Medicare patients. More organizations will likely be certified in 2014.

A key component to the success of these organizations is the ability to share data and information. Without such an ability to share information, it is doubtful that these organizations would be able to meet their goal of improving quality and reducing cost.

ACOs are required to collect and interpret data to promote quality and cost efficiency. An ACO collects clinical information from a variety of sources, analyzes the data, and develops appropriate clinical protocols. A properly functioning ACO analyzes cost trends to determine the most efficient treatment for the patient population to be served by the ACO.

The reality is that ACOs require the collection and sharing of extensive medical data, both demographic and clinical. A good data system can make the ACO efficient, while a bad system will result in the ACO working blind. Without data and accessibility, the ACO is attempting a formation landing in dense fog. Data is the guidance that will bring the flight in safely.

While the advantages of ACOs have been hotly debated, the potential exposure if the data is not kept secure, has not been given much attention. Nevertheless, the amount of data that must be shared, analyzed, and transmitted creates the potential for unprecedented liability for both accidental and intentional misuse. This chapter discusses some of those risks and the steps ACOs and providers need to take to protect themselves from such risks.

While this chapter focuses on ACOs, the concepts are applicable to any clinically integrated healthcare practice. Integration is the touchstone of an ACO. While not all clinically integrated organizations are ACOs, all ACOs must be clinically integrated.[1] Moreover, the insurance exchanges created by the Affordable Care Act create many opportunities for the misuse of

---

[1] In this respect, the Federal Trade Commission and Department of Justice consider any approved ACO to be deemed clinically integrated such to justify rule of reason treatment under the antitrust laws and to allow joint negotiation with commercial payers. *See* Statement of Antitrust Enforcement Policy Regarding Accountable Care Organizations Participating in the Medicare Shared Savings Program, 76 Fed. R. 67026 (Oct. 28, 2011).

consumer data as consumers apply for coverage through the web-based portals. The Department of Health and Human Services (HHS), along with the Department of Justice and Federal Trade Commission (FTC), has identified the potential for fraud in enrolling consumers in exchange-based health plans as an ongoing concern.[2]

ACO Requirements Under Shared Savings Program

Most ACOs will endeavor to become part of the Medicare Shared Savings program. To qualify under the program, an ACO must be a legal entity formed under applicable state, federal, or tribal law and authorized to conduct business in each state where it operates. It must maintain an identifiable governing body with authority to execute its functions including, but not limited to, the promotion of evidence-based medicine and reporting on quality and cost measures. Under the rules, the ACO governing body is responsible for the oversight and strategic direction of the ACO. The following entities may qualify to become an ACO:

- Professionals in group practice arrangements;
- Networks of individual practices of ACO professionals;
- Partnerships or joint venture arrangements between hospitals and ACO professionals;
- Hospitals employing ACO professionals;
- Certain critical access hospitals;
- Rural health centers; and
- Federally qualified health centers.

The ACO must have at least 5,000 assigned Medicare beneficiaries. This is determined by the number of beneficiaries historically assigned to ACO participants in each of the three years before the start of the agreement with CMS to enter the shared savings program. In cases where the ACO's assigned population falls below 5,000, it will be issued a warning and placed on a Corrective Action Plan (CAP). Falling below the required number of beneficiaries will also result in a reduction in the savings the ACO may recoup.

---

[2] *See* Press Release, Centers for Medicare and Medicaid Services, Securing the Health Insurance Marketplace, Sept. 18, 2013, http://www.cms.gov/Newsroom/MediaReleaseDatabase/Fact-Sheets/2013-Fact-Sheets-Items/2013-09-18.html.

Importantly, the ACO is required to promote and adopt evidence-based medicine guidelines and report to CMS on quality and cost metrics. In this regard, a qualified healthcare professional must be responsible for the Quality Assurance and Improvement Program, and the ACO must explain in its application how it will require participants and providers to comply with and implement the policies.

The functions and goals of the ACO are articulated in CMS's requirements for ACO policies. The ACO must define, establish, and implement policies to accomplish the following:

- Promote evidence-based medicine that covers diagnosis with significant potential for the ACO to achieve quality improvements.
- Promote patient engagement, including compliance with patient experience surveys and a process for evaluating the health needs of the population.
- Development of an infrastructure for participants and providers to report on quality.
- Coordinate care across and among primary care physicians, specialists, and acute care providers.

ACOs must agree to participate in the program for at least three years.

A significant aspect of an ACO participating in the shared savings program is the measurement of quality after a range of categories. The final regulations include thirty separate measures over four general domains that will be analyzed:

- Patient/caregiver experience (seven measures)
- Care coordination/patient safety (six measures)
- Preventive health (eight measures)
- At-risk populations (twelve measures)

An ACO's score on each measure determines the amount of shared savings it may receive. This score is calculated by adding the points earned on each individual measure within the specific domain. For the first year of performance, an ACO will be deemed to have met the performance requirements if it provides the necessary data to CMS. In subsequent years, quality performance standards will be phased in based upon the minimal attainment level for certain measures. Performance will be judged on a sliding scale from 200 to the maximum points allowed for such measure.

ACOs that fail to meet the minimum standard will not receive a score for the particular measure. To achieve a maximum score, the ACO must perform at or above the ninetieth percentile of the benchmark.

Although the final regulations did not require that all participants in the ACO become a "meaningful user" of electronic health record (EHR) technology, it is clear that any ACO must have a robust data system to manage the risk and achieve the cost savings requirement to receive a share of the savings. One of the measures contained in the care coordination domain is the use of an EHR system by primary care physicians.

In addition to the unprecedented amount of information that ACO participants must share with each other, a considerable amount of information is being shared between CMS and the ACO. This creates the potential for additional exposure to the ACO and its participants if there is a breach of the system. Moreover, as information sharing is critical to the ability of the ACO to achieve its goals, the information will likely be shared widely, thereby further increasing the possibility that a participant somewhere along the chain will suffer a breach. In essence, the entire security of the ACO is only as strong as the weakest link in the member network.

Challenges Posed by ACOs

Information Sharing

One of the hallmark components of an ACO is the ability to share information among providers at various levels of the care continuum. For example, primary care physicians must have the ability to access and share information with specialists and upstream providers such as hospitals. This naturally requires a robust and interoperable electronic health record. While the concept of an interoperable health record predates the formal adoption of the ACO concept as contained in the Medicare shared savings program, interoperability among ACO members is vital to the function of the ACO.

In fact, the participation in the shared savings program requires that the ACO freely share medical data:

> (c) The ACO must not limit or restrict appropriate sharing of medical record data with providers and suppliers both within and outside the ACO in accordance with applicable law.[3]

One of the central problems with ACO formation is that implementation is difficult for providers that are not fully integrated. The systems that are usually touted as being "integrated" are typically those systems that employ physicians and otherwise have control over the practices. Most health systems, however, function on an independent staff physician model whereby the physicians are not employed by the health system itself. As a result, there is less control over the practice, and especially the employees working at such practices. In most circumstances, the ACO would have no ability to discipline employees of the physician for practices that may violate the privacy of ACO patients. Nevertheless, the ACO could be held liable for the actions of the physician's office if there is a breach.

Clinical Integration

Clinical integration is a central function of any ACO. While all ACOs will be clinically integrated, not all clinically integrated networks are ACOs in either the traditional sense or in the formal Medicare Shared Savings sense.

Most of the definition of "clinical" integration comes from advisory opinions from the FTC, where the issue of whether a network is clinically integrated determines whether it will be subject to rule of reason treatment under the antitrust laws or whether it will be deemed a price-fixing cartel where it is subject to per se condemnation under the federal antitrust laws.[4]

---

[3] 42 C.F.R. § 425.700 (West).

[4] Although beyond the scope of this chapter, the central issue is whether the network is a valid "joint venture" or a collection of independent providers agreeing to price or price-related terms. The latter would constitute a "conspiracy" to restrain trade under Section 1 of the Sherman Antitrust Act, 15, U.S.C. § 1. An agreement on price is deemed to be price fixing, which is considered to be "per se" unlawful under Section 1. In other words, the participants are precluded from justifying the reasons for the conduct. A joint venture is analyzed under the "rule of reason" where the pro-competitive justifications are balanced against the anticompetitive conduct.

The FTC's MedSouth advisory opinion provides insight as to this requirement, given it is essential that the network have a degree of stability, thereby making it necessary for the network to engage in joint contracting.

To establish and maintain the ongoing collaboration and interdependence among physicians from which the projected efficiencies flow, the doctors need to be able to rely on the participation of other members of the group in the network on a continuing basis. This does not appear to be possible if contracting for the sale of services is done individually. The price for professional services rendered under health plan contracts needs to be established, and if it is done through individual negotiation and contracting, then no one can count on the full participation of the group's members. Whatever value the program has for consumers, beyond what would result from individual doctors computerizing their records and determining to follow particular guidelines, is significantly dependent on the doctors being able to function as a group within which patients are commonly referred. In the absence of the group being able to ensure continuing participation of its members in its contracts, some of the benefits are likely to go unrealized.

The real question is whether the ACO can articulate a strategy for joint contracting. In most cases, it should be able to. First, one of the key components of an ACO is the ability to move away from fee-for-service contracting. To fully achieve the goals of lowering cost and improving quality (i.e., promoting accountability), an ACO must negotiate jointly for a bundled rate. In fact, it would defeat the purpose of accountable care if the ACO attempted to negotiate separate rates for core participants. Thus, the very structure of an ACO demands some form of joint contracting. In fact, meaningful gains to lower cost and improve quality cannot happen without bundled contracts.[5]

Some of the keys to integration are as follows:

- A collaborative network of primary care physicians and specialists to provide care in a seamless, coordinated manner;

---

[5] Letter from Jeffrey W. Brennan to John J. Miles, Ober, Kaler, Grimes & Shriver, dated February 19, 2002 (Medsouth), available at http://www.ftc.gov/bc/adops/medsouth.shtm.

- Collaboration of providers in designing, implementing, and applying evidence-based practice guidelines and monitoring performance to improve patient care and reduce costs;
- Integration of physicians and providers of medical services in the community through a web-based electronic health record; and
- Decrease the overall administrative regulatory burden by reducing paperwork and time needed to process treatment information.[6]

The EHR system proposed in Greater Rochester Independent Practice Association (GRIPA) consisted of the following:

- Referral and consultation notes;
- Drug prescriptions;
- Lab orders and results, diagnostic imaging reports, and links to actual images; and
- Hospital inpatient and outpatient information such as discharge summaries, instructions, consulting physician reports, and hospital diagnostic reports.[7]

The initial proposed ACO regulations would have required that ACO participants become "meaningful users" of EHR systems. This requirement was dropped as it might have prevented some physicians from joining ACOs. Nevertheless, a robust EHR would be vital to the success of the ACO and utilization of an EHR is one factor that is used to evaluate an ACO.[8]

Access to Medicare Data

In addition to the flow of information horizontally among members of the ACO, there is a considerable amount of information that will flow between the ACO and payers, such as Medicare. To this end, an ACO must be able to monitor both costs and patient care very closely as the ability to save under the programs requires a delicate balance between providing all

[6] Federal Trade Commission, Advisory Opinion, Greater Rochester Independent Practice Association, Inc., at 5-6, Sept. 17, 2007, http://www.ftc.gov/bc/adops/gripa.pdf.

[7] *Id.* at 7.

[8] The final rules only adopted measure 20, which requires reporting on EHR use. See Table 1 to Interim Final Rule. The final rule measures how many physicians are eligible for incentive payments under the EHR incentive program.

necessary services while at the same time providing care in the most efficient manner possible.

Under the shared savings program, CMS may provide the following type of data, shared as aggregate reports with ACOs as follows:

a. Aggregate reports are shared at the start of the agreement period based on beneficiary claims data used to calculate the benchmark, and each quarter thereafter during the agreement period.
b. These aggregate reports include, when available, the following information, de-identified in accordance with 45 CFR 164.514(b):

    i. Aggregated metrics on the assigned beneficiary population.
    ii. Utilization and expenditure data at the start of the agreement period based on historical beneficiaries used to calculate the benchmark.

c. At the beginning of the agreement period, during each quarter (and in conjunction with the annual reconciliation), and at the beginning of each performance year, CMS, upon the ACO's request for the data for purposes of population-based activities relating to improving health or reducing growth in health care costs, process development, case management, and care coordination, will provide the ACO with information regarding preliminarily prospectively assigned beneficiaries whose data was used to generate the aggregate data reports under paragraphs (a) and (b) of this section. The information includes the following:

    i. Beneficiary name;
    ii. Date of birth;
    iii. HICN; and
    iv. Sex

d. In its request for these data, the ACO must certify that it is seeking the following information:

    i. As a HIPAA-covered entity, and the request reflects the minimum data necessary for the ACO to conduct its own health care operations work that falls within the first or second paragraph of the definition of health care operations at 45 CFR 164.501.

ii. As the business associate of its ACO participants and ACO providers/suppliers, who are HIPAA-covered entities, and the request reflects the minimum data necessary for the ACO to conduct health care operations work that falls within the first or second paragraph of the definition of health care operations at 45 CFR 164.501 on behalf of those participants.[9]

Given the potential for the sharing of Protected Health Information (PHI) regarding beneficiaries, any ACO wishing to receive data from CMS must sign a data-sharing agreement, which is essentially an agreement to comply with HIPAA. Violating the agreement, however, will result in the ACO's forfeiting of its right to receive the data and the ACO could be terminated from the Shared Savings program:

(1) Before receiving any beneficiary identifiable data, ACOs must enter into a DUA (Data Use Agreement) with CMS. Under the DUA, the ACO must comply with the limitations on use and disclosure imposed by HIPAA, the applicable DUA, and the statutory and regulatory requirements of the Shared Savings Program.

(2) If the ACO misuses or discloses data in a manner that violates any applicable statutory or regulatory requirements or that is otherwise non-compliant with the provisions of the DUA, it will no longer be eligible to receive data under subpart H of this part, may be terminated from the Shared Savings Program under §425.218, and may be subject to additional sanctions and penalties available under the law.[10]

Information must be shared among ACO participants to meaningfully change behavior and increase quality. Thus, it is conceivable that members will have access to the data. Although the information may be provided in aggregate form, it is still conceivable that there will be PHI in the information. Here, it is essential for the ACO to encrypt the information and develop strong policies regarding such encryption. This can be the key to avoiding penalties under The Health Information Technology for

[9] 42 C.F.R. § 425.702 (West).
[10] 42 C.F.R. § 425.710 (West).

Economic and Clinical Health Act (HITECH), as encrypted information is considered secured.[11]

New HITECH Breach Standard and Application of HIPAA Rules

In January 2013, CMS published its long-awaited Final Omnibus Rules, which implemented portions of HITECH. HITECH, among other things, provided for significant civil penalties for violations of HIPAA and made the security and privacy requirements of HIPAA applicable to business associates. Hence, both providers (covered entities) and organizations that provide services on behalf of those entities, i.e., consultants, attorneys, (deemed business associates) are now required to comply with HIPAA if their work requires that they have access to patient information.

One of the major changes to HITECH enforcement rules was the threshold for determining a breach. Previously, the HITECH interim regulations applied a balancing test whereby the covered entity had to assess whether the breach possessed a significant risk of financial, reputational, or other harm to the individual whose records were the subject of the breach. Under the new regulations, a breach is presumed unless the covered entity or business associate can demonstrate that there is a low probability that the protected health information has been compromised based on an analysis of the following factors:

1. The nature and extent of the protected health information involved, including the types of identifiers and the likelihood of re-identification;
2. The unauthorized person who used the protected health information or to whom the disclosure was made;
3. Whether the protected health information was actually acquired or viewed; and
4. The extent to which the risk to the protected health information has been mitigated.

[11] Notification of patients is required only when there is a breach of "unsecured" information. 45 C.F.R. §164.404 (West). Unsecured information is defined as information that is not rendered unusable, unreadable, or indecipherable to unauthorized individuals through use of a technology or methodology approved by CMS. For electronic data, this means encryption. *See* 45 C.F.R. §164.402 (West).

Where the breach involves more than 500 patients, the covered entity or business associate is required to notify the Office of Civil Rights and the media of the breach. This will undoubtedly result in an inquiry. The publicity, not to mention the threat of fines, is a significant reason to be extra vigilant in protecting health information.

HIPAA Compliance and Security Audits

The Office of Civil Rights (OCR) has become increasingly active in fining practices for HIPAA violations. Physician offices remain a focus of those efforts. In this regard, on April 17, 2012, it levied a $100,000 fine against a cardiac practice in Phoenix that came under investigation after it posted clinical and surgical appointments for its patients on an Internet-based calendar that was publicly accessible. On further investigation, OCR discovered that the practice had implemented few policies and procedures to comply with the HIPAA Privacy and Security Rules, and had limited safeguards in place to protect patients' electronic protected health information (ePHI). Notably, OCR concluded:

1. Phoenix Cardiac Surgery failed to implement adequate policies and procedures to appropriately safeguard patient information;
2. Phoenix Cardiac Surgery failed to document that it trained any employees on its policies and procedures on the privacy and security rules;
3. Phoenix Cardiac Surgery failed to identify a security official and conduct a risk analysis; and
4. Phoenix Cardiac Surgery failed to obtain business associate agreements with Internet-based e-mail and calendar services where the provision of the service included storage of and access to its ePHI.

It is important that the ACO have policies in place to monitor compliance with HIPAA security and privacy regulations. An audit of compliance at hospitals conducted by the Office of Inspector General revealed multiple compliance issues with the HIPAA security regulations. Specifically, the report noted that "audits of 7 hospitals throughout the United States identified 151 vulnerabilities in the systems and controls intended to protect ePHI, of which 124 were categorized as high impact. These vulnerabilities placed the confidentiality, integrity, and availability of ePHI at risk. Outsiders or employees at some hospitals could have accessed, and at one hospital did access, systems and beneficiaries' personal data and performed unauthorized acts without the hospitals' knowledge." These were deemed to be "high impact" vulnerabilities which the study defined as those that:

- may result in the highly costly loss of major tangible assets or resources;
- may significantly violate, harm, or impede an organization's mission, reputation, or interest; or
- may result in human death or serious injury.

The audits were conducted at hospitals in California, Georgia, Illinois, Massachusetts, Missouri, New York, and Texas, and focused on the hospitals' implementation of:

- the wireless electronic communications network or security measures the security management staff implemented in its computerized information systems (technical safeguards);
- the physical access to electronic information systems and the facilities in which they are housed (physical safeguards); and
- the policies and procedures developed and implemented for the security measures to protect the confidentiality, integrity, and availability of ePHI (administrative safeguards).

The OIG concluded that:

> Although OCR stated that it maintains a process for initiating covered entity compliance reviews in the absence of complaints, it provided no evidence that it had actually done so. The only reviews OCR mentioned were related to our hospital audits. In the absence of evidence of a more expansive review process, we encourage OCR to continue the compliance review process begun by CMS in 2009.

Consistent with the criticisms, OCR began auditing providers for all aspects of HIPAA compliance. To this end, OCR established a comprehensive audit protocol that contains the requirements to be assessed through these performance audits. The audit process is organized around modules, representing separate elements of privacy, security, and breach notification. According to OCR:

a. The audit protocol covers Privacy Rule requirements for (1) notice of privacy practices for PHI, (2) rights to request privacy protection for PHI, (3) access of individuals to PHI, (4) administrative requirements, (5) uses and disclosures of PHI, (6) amendment of PHI, and (7) accounting of disclosures.
b. The protocol covers Security Rule requirements for administrative, physical, and technical safeguards.
c. The protocol covers requirements for the Breach Notification Rule.

Given that OCR intends to audit providers, it is a good idea to perform a self-audit of ACO participants. While the HIPAA security regulations require that a covered entity perform periodic audits, in practice, such audits are rarely conducted and when they are, they are far from comprehensive. Thus, as a starting point, the ACO should require that the participant disclose its HIPAA policies and provide information as to the last time a security audit was performed by the entity.

As the ACO could potentially be liable for a breach, the ACO must itself ensure that the members are compliant with the security regulations, and this would also involve an audit by the ACO of HIPAA security issues. Finally, the ACO will want the participants to disclose any past breaches to determine whether steps were taken to prevent such breaches in the future. As most insurers now offer some type of data breach coverage as a stand-alone product or as an add-on to an existing policy, the ACO should consider purchasing such insurance.

Potential Damages/Fines for A Breach

While providing proper training is no defense to the civil sanctions that may be imposed as a result of a data breach, demonstrating that the ACO provided mandatory recurrent training can mitigate the potential for civil fines if a breach does occur. Under the HITECH Act, fines vary depending on the degree of culpability. However, penalties are determined by multiplying the number of records times the number of separate HIPAA violations. In this regard, the numbers can add up quickly for a large breach. The fines are tiered as follows:

- Unknowing Violations—$100 per violation ($1.5k max)
- Reasonable Cause—$1,000 per violation ($1.5k max)
- Willful Neglect (corrected)—$10,000 ($1.5k max)
- Willful Neglect (uncorrected)—$50,000 ($1.5M max)

In addition to the potential for fines, the ACO faces the specter of a civil suit for negligence. While there is no private cause of action under HIPAA, the HIPAA regulations, as well as state law, can constitute the standard of care for a breach. In *Resnick v. AvMed, Inc.*, the eleventh Circuit Court of Appeals allowed a complaint to proceed where the plaintiff alleged that a health plan was negligent in not maintaining the security of two laptop computers that contained unencrypted PHI, Social Security Numbers, names, addresses, and phone numbers.[12] The computers contained information about approximately 1.2 million members. After the theft, fraudulent bank accounts and credit cards were issued in the names of the named plaintiffs.

Finding that the plaintiffs set forth a reasonable nexus between the theft of the laptop computer and the negligence of AvMed in failing to protect the computer, the court held that the plaintiffs had pled an injury in fact under the law. Unlike claims of the mere threat of harm, the court held that to prove that a data breach caused identity theft, the pleadings must show a nexus between the two instances beyond allegations of time and sequence. The fact that the plaintiffs had guarded their information by destroying sensitive materials and not been the subject of prior identity thefts added the facts necessary to establish the causal nexus. These facts, concluded the court, rose to the minimum level to conclude that it was plausible that the theft was the cause of the identity theft. The court, however, refused to let stand the claim that the alleged violation of Florida law constituted negligence per se.

Risk Assessment and Management

While the potential for a data breach in an ACO is magnified by the number of participants and the lack of overall control over the independent groups, such potential can be managed by good HIPAA security practices and monitoring of the participants.

---

[12] *Resnick v. AvMed, Inc.*, 693 F.3d 1317 (11th Cir. 2012).

Audit of Security at ACO Participants

An ACO should conduct periodic audits of the security practices of all participants. This is a requirement of the HIPAA security rules, but often, audits are merely cursory and do not drill down sufficiently to determine current threats.

HIPAA security standards require the following:

a. Risk analysis (Required). Conduct an accurate and thorough assessment of the potential risks and vulnerabilities to the confidentiality, integrity, and availability of electronic protected health information held by the covered entity.
b. Risk management (Required). Implement security measures sufficient to reduce risks and vulnerabilities to a reasonable and appropriate level to comply with §164.306(a).
c. Sanction policy (Required). Apply appropriate sanctions against workforce members who fail to comply with the security policies and procedures of the covered entity.
d. Information system activity review (Required). Implement procedures to regularly review records of information system activity, such as audit logs, access reports, and security incident tracking reports.[13]

Unfortunately, at many physician offices, HIPAA is a "done it and forget it" type of policy. ACO management should require that each member have a current audit.[14] Better yet, the ACO itself should retain a consultant to perform random audits of its members. In my experience, it is better to have this audit preformed by an entity that does not currently maintain the computer systems for a provider. Such audits by existing vendors are often cursory and do not assess the real threat to the provider and the ACO.

Appointment of Privacy and Security Officers by ACO

The ACO should consider appointment of its own privacy and security officers to oversee these functions. While many ACOs will be hospital or

---

[13] 45 C.F.R. 164.308(a)(1)(ii).

[14] 45 C.F.R. 164.306(e) provides that "Security measures must be reviewed and modified to ensure the continued protection of electronic PHI." 45 C.F.R. 164.306(e)."

large-practice driven, it is important that to the extent the ACO consists of non-employed practices that there be a mechanism to address privacy and security issues. At first, this may seem duplicative if the ACO was developed by a large organization. However, for efficiency and accountability purposes, the ACO should have an individual who is independent from the provider to assess and address privacy and security issues.

As the ACO will have its own governance structure, it is reasonable to require some independence from the privacy and security officers, especially given the different network focus of the ACO. This recommendation would apply regardless of whether the ACO itself is a covered entity for HIPAA purposes, or whether it is deemed to be a business associate of member-covered entities. Either way, the security issues facing the ACO are separate and distinct from the concerns of the members themselves. The more independent the members are from each other, the greater the need to monitor overall compliance.

Creation of ACO-Specific Policies

Finally, ACOs must be viewed as separate entities from their component member organizations. While the goal is to have the independent groups function as an integrated unit, the individual members may not always have sufficient information to analyze the risk of the ACO as a whole. Moreover, while related, the member provider's security and privacy issues may be slightly different from those of the ACO.

In essence, the ACO must oversee the entire network. Expecting that the providers are able to oversee the entire ACO may result in an inability to focus on the big picture. In the vernacular, the providers may be unable to see the forest (the ACO) from the ground level of providing care to beneficiaries. This does not mean that all ACO member security can be handled by the ACO. Again, the focus of the ACO is on the overall function of the ACO, not the individual practice level. The ACO may suffer from its own inability to see the trees (the day-to-day individual issues) because of its focus on the overall network.

Conclusion

ACOs have the potential to increase efficiencies while reducing costs through the coordination of care. Data access and data sharing are central to the functionality of the ACO. The data systems that will be necessary to implement an effective ACO are in the emergent stage, and as few ACOs are up and running, it remains to be seen how the data systems will evolve. Importantly, HIT needs to become more involved in ACO implementation. Surprisingly, few HIT departments at institutional providers such as hospitals are involved in these discussions. While this will change by necessity, ACOs will encounter a good bit of "growing pains" once they are up and running.

A good start, however, is to think about HIPAA issues during the formation, and to work proactively in assessing these risks. An ACO that is reactive and assumes that all of its members are conversant in HIPAA issues could find itself in deep trouble. Privacy in an ACO is only as strong as the weakest practice in the ACO.

Key Takeaways

- In theory, information in an ACO must flow in real time over an unimpeded pipeline. This flow of information is vital if the ACO is to achieve the goal of providing higher quality care and reduced costs. This is the central thrust of the Accountable Care Organization.
- The amount of data that must be shared, analyzed, and transmitted by ACOs creates the potential for unprecedented liability for both accidental and intentional misuse.
- To fully achieve the goals of lowering cost and improving quality (i.e., promoting accountability), an ACO must create an appropriate mechanism to share savings so as to incentivize the participants. Many of the lessons learned from clinically integrated organizations will apply.
- It is essential for the ACO to develop strong policies regarding privacy and security, including appropriate encryption protocols. This can be the key to avoiding penalties under the Health Information Technology for Economic and Clinical Health Act, as encrypted information is considered secured.
- ACOs must be viewed as separate entities from their component member organizations. While related, the member provider's security and privacy issues may be slightly different from those of the ACO.

Mark Mattioli chairs the Health Law Practice Group and the Health Care Governmental Compliance Practice Group, and is also co-chair of the Privacy and Data Security Practice Group at Marshall Dennehey Warner Coleman and Goggin. Mr. Mattioli provides regulatory, transactional, and compliance guidance to hospitals, physicians, and other health care providers in a variety of areas, including health care reform, managed care contracting, reimbursement, fraud and abuse (Stark and anti-kickback), health information privacy and security, medical staff credentialing, and antitrust. Mr. Mattioli routinely advises hospitals, health care systems, and providers regarding government audits, government payment programs, medical staff issues, and electronic discovery, as well as privacy and data security matters. Mr. Mattioli has extensive experience in consulting with health care clients and in litigating matters in health law and other highly regulated industries.

Technology Complicates Privacy Compliance

Brenda R. Sharton

Partner

Goodwin Procter LLP

ASPATORE

Introduction

The privacy landscape continues to change as technology advances. Growing use of digital media, cloud computing, social networking, and mobile devices has exponentially increased the information collection practices throughout the world, fueled in part by the growth in behavioral advertising and target marketing. As more personal information is collected, collated, and analyzed, there has been increased focus on privacy protections and transparency. Government regulators are paying close attention, and we have seen a rise in government investigations and enforcement actions. In particular, the Federal Trade Commission (FTC) has shown greater willingness to use its broad authority under Section 5 of the FTC Act to ensure that companies fulfill the privacy and data security promises they make to consumers. Moreover, in the medical sector, the US Department of Health and Services has implemented an audit program to examine health information privacy risks and compliance efforts across the industry.

As a result of these trends, we have seen companies become increasingly focused on and sophisticated about privacy issues. Many businesses now handle privacy issues internally that were once left to outside counsel and consultants. Individuals in key management positions are also becoming more sophisticated regarding technological advancements and the associated privacy concerns. So-called "privacy by design" (i.e., building privacy protections into products and services at the outset) is now becoming more commonplace as companies begin to fully comprehend the benefits and pitfalls of the new digital age.

Gramm-Leach-Bliley Act's Effect on Information Security

The Gramm-Leach-Bliley (GLB) Act has had a significant impact in the privacy and data security realm. Although the GLB Act's reach is limited to financial institutions that store and share "nonpublic personal information," it has established a benchmark for the way companies across a wide array of industries inform consumers about company privacy practices and protect personal information.

First, the GLB Act's implementing regulations require financial institutions to provide customers with "clear and conspicuous" written notices describing their privacy policies and practices as well as a reasonable opportunity to opt out of information sharing with non-affiliated third parties. The GLB Act thus codified in federal law the notice and opt-out regime, which has become the standard governing privacy practice in the United States.

The other hallmark of the GLB Act is its requirement that financial institutions safeguard personal information against unauthorized access and disclosure, the so-called Safeguards Rule. Under the Safeguards Rule, the GLB Act requires implementation of written information security programs to ensure the security and confidentiality of personal information. Many of the Safeguards Rule requirements, such as risk assessment, service provider oversight, compliance monitoring, and employee training, are now found in other federal and state data security laws.

The GLB Act also sets forth an important data security standard: Information security programs must be tailored to each company's risks, size, and the scope of their information collection and use practices. This "one size does not fit all" approach remains a cornerstone of data security across all businesses. Companies cannot simply copy each other's programs. Attorneys thus play an important role in ensuring that businesses conduct the appropriate risk assessments and due diligence, and then in customizing safeguards suitable to the circumstances.

Cloud Computing Challenges

Cloud computing has been at the forefront of privacy discussions in recent years. Cloud computing offers companies potentially significant IT and administrative cost savings by allowing users to store and manage data on third party-operated remote computer networks. Despite the meaningful benefits such outsourcing can bring, companies are still required to comply with applicable privacy and data security laws and remain legally responsible for data stored in the cloud. By placing data in the hands of a third party, cloud computing presents additional risks.

For companies using or considering cloud computing, the service contract with the cloud provider is key. One significant challenge companies face is that cloud providers typically offer standard form agreements that provide basic and minimum data security protections. Companies should consult with their attorneys in negotiating these agreements to better protect information in the cloud. In particular, companies should be wary of contracts from vendors that offer vague assurances of "reasonable" security. Outside counsel can help draft stronger data security provisions that specify security requirements and ensure that a cloud provider's security measures will be in compliance with any relevant privacy laws and regulations. Contracts should also address breach notification obligations and, if possible, provide for indemnification in the event of a data breach. Moreover, companies should make sure to do their due diligence before engaging any service provider to confirm that the provider is capable of safeguarding data in accordance with applicable law.

One other important aspect of cloud computing that companies need to consider relates to electronic surveillance. Information stored in the cloud is subject to different privacy protections and may be at greater risk of compelled disclosure to the government. For instance, the US Supreme Court, in *United States v. Miller*, a case involving disclosure of a customer's bank records to the government pursuant to subpoenas issued by the government, held that the Fourth Amendment, which forbids unreasonable searches and seizures, does not prohibit obtaining of information revealed to a third party and that there was no constitutionally protected privacy interest in records held by the bank.[1] In addition, under the Electronic Communications Privacy Act (ECPA), information stored on "remote computing services" for more than 180 days may be subject to government search through a subpoena rather than a warrant. More recently, cloud computing services have been caught in the middle of the controversy involving the National Security Agency's electronic surveillance program (known as PRISM), leading many cloud customers to move away from US-based cloud providers toward international providers that are not subject to such surveillance.

Privacy and Data Security Compliance Challenges

The privacy regime in the United States is typically referred to as a "patchwork quilt" of regulation. While federal regulation generally addresses sector and information-specific privacy concerns, (e.g., financial,

---

[1] *U.S. v. Miller*, 425 U.S. 435 (1976).

health, children) state data security laws serve to fill in some of the gaps and tend to be broader, although geographically limited. For companies doing business nationwide, complying with the varied and often overlapping data security laws can be challenging.

California has often been at the forefront in terms of developing privacy and data security laws, and, in fact, many California laws have set the standard for state regulation throughout the United States. Take, for example, California's 2004 Online Privacy Protection Act, which was the first state law requiring websites to post a privacy policy describing the kinds of information collected by the website and how the information may be shared with third parties. Although the law governs websites that collect personal information of California residents, most website operators apply the law to all data collection from consumers, whether California residents or not.

State legislatures have been particularly cognizant of the rise of identity theft and data security breaches involving companies of all sizes, across all industries. Accordingly, forty-six states, the District of Columbia, and Puerto Rico have adopted breach notification laws requiring prompt disclosure of data breaches to affected individuals. Once again, California was the first state to pass such a law in 2002, thereby providing the roadmap for nearly every other state to follow. However, states have started to look to more proactive measures to protect personal information, and some have enacted increasingly stringent data security requirements. The state leading this charge has been Massachusetts.

In 2009, Massachusetts enacted strict and detailed data security regulations to govern entities possessing personal information of Massachusetts residents. Massachusetts requires companies that hold personal information about its residents to implement written information security programs and security procedures for storing and sharing personal information. Among its many requirements, the most problematic mandates of the Massachusetts rules involve encryption and oversight of third-party service providers. Specifically, they require encryption of all personal information stored on portable devices (such as laptops, smartphones, and flash drives) and transmitted on public or wireless networks. The rules also compel companies to select service providers that are capable of maintaining safeguards for personal information consistent with the Massachusetts requirements and to contractually require service providers to maintain such safeguards.

The effect of the rules has been wide-reaching since the regulations apply to any entity possessing personal information of Massachusetts residents. While companies in other heavily regulated industries such as financial services and health care companies may be well-positioned to comply, these regulations have raised the bar for entities not normally accustomed to tackling such comprehensive data security issues. In particular, smaller entities with reduced IT capabilities, including small businesses and non-profits, have struggled with the increased costs and obligations associated with compliance. Outside counsel with experience and expertise in developing information security policies are an invaluable resource for entities seeking to attain compliance.

Recent Significant Privacy and Data Security Court Cases

The US Supreme Court recently issued an important decision regarding standing to sue for alleged privacy violations. In *Clapper v. Amnesty International USA*, the Court ruled that journalists/human rights activists/labor leaders had no Article III standing to challenge 2008 amendments to Foreign Intelligence Surveillance Act (FISA).[2] FISA permits warrantless monitoring of electronic communications of non-US persons overseas. Plaintiffs in *Clapper* argued that they were forced to pay more to communicate with their clients and were fearful that their communications were being monitored under FISA. The Court held to establish standing based on the risk of future harm, plaintiffs must show that the threatened injury is "certainly impending." The Court also rejected plaintiffs' argument that they suffered injury by incurring costs to avoid FISA surveillance.

The implications of the Supreme Court's decision go well beyond FISA and government surveillance. Specifically, *Clapper* may help companies defending against data breach (class action) litigation by bolstering arguments that plaintiffs can neither depend on a hypothetical fear of future injury, such as potential future identity theft, nor rely on manufactured injury, such as costs incurred for credit monitoring, to establish standing to sue.

[2] *Clapper v. Amnesty International USA*, 133 S. Ct. 1138 (2013).

Nevertheless, in class actions involving unlawful interception or disclosure of electronic communications under the ECPA, the effect of *Clapper* may be more limited. In general, the ECPA protects wire, oral, and electronic communications, including e-mail, telephone conversations, and data stored electronically while such communications are being made, when they are in transit, and when they are stored on computers. Whereas in *Clapper,* the plaintiffs did not allege that their communications were intercepted, plaintiffs in other cases have been able to establish standing by demonstrating that their personal information was accessed without consent. For example, in *Dunstan v. comScore, Inc.*, a federal district court in the northern district of Illinois recently certified a class of plaintiffs alleging that comScore software tracked and collected private information from users' computers without notice or authorization.[3] The Seventh Circuit subsequently denied comScore's petition to appeal the class certification ruling.

In the retail sphere, a recent decision by Massachusetts' highest court, *Tyler v. Michaels Stores, Inc.*, significantly affects retailers operating in Massachusetts that collect personal information during credit card transactions.[4] The court interpreted key provisions of a Massachusetts consumer privacy statute limiting what "personal identification information" may be collected during a card transaction, and concluded, among other things, that a consumer's zip code is "personal identification information" under that statute. Consequently, retailers that collect zip codes during payment card transactions may be violating Massachusetts law. This decision follows a California Supreme Court case, *Pineda v. Williams-Sonoma,* similarly holding that zip codes constitute "personal information" under California law.[5]

Approaches to Data Management and Security

In general, companies should take a three-prong approach to data management and data security: assessment and investigation, risk-management, and compliance monitoring. To begin, before any company or organization can fully address data security issues, it must first understand the full scope of its data collection and use practices as well as the attendant risks. This is the assessment and investigation phase. A company needs to know

[3] *Harris v. comScore,* April 2, 2013.
[4] *Tyler v. Michaels Stores, Inc.*, 464 Mass. 492 (2013).
[5] *Pineda v. Williams-Sonoma, Inc.*, 51 Cal. 4th 524 (Cal. 2011).

exactly what types of data it collects, how it collects the data, and where the data resides. A company also needs to fully understand how the data will be used and who will or may have access to the data, both internally and externally. We therefore work closely with our clients to conduct internal privacy reviews, examine internal use of data and use of data by third parties, and analyze data storage and retention practices to chart the data flow and identify potential risks to data security.

Once clients better understand their data collection and use practices, they can then focus on risk-management and mitigation. The development of robust privacy and information security policies that outline suitable security safeguards and providing guidelines for appropriate use of information in compliance with the myriad privacy laws are the minimum. IT departments should implement necessary technical, physical, and administrative security measures. It is also prudent to develop crisis management and incident response plans designed to minimize harm resulting from data breaches. Waiting until the breach occurs will result in precious time being wasted figuring out what needs to be done next. Having the plan in place beforehand is critical to a fast and less pressured response. In addition, pay special attention to service providers to ensure that their practices are consistent with your policies and also in compliance with applicable laws. Managing service providers by auditing vendor security policies and revising vendor agreements to help minimize client liability is an important part of the process.

Lastly, companies need to actively monitor their information policies and practices to ensure compliance on an ongoing basis. It is prudent to conduct periodic privacy audits and risk assessments, regularly review privacy policies, and continually train employees and staff. It is also important that clients stay informed about the evolving legal and regulatory environment by monitoring proposed legislation as well as relevant litigation and enforcement actions.

Best Practices for Protecting Data in Transit and in Storage

For the most part, privacy regulation in the United States has been technology-neutral as lawmakers have been reluctant to mandate specific technology practices. However, as identity theft and data security breaches continue to plague consumers, regulators are starting to take notice of certain practices. In particular, we have seen that encryption is quickly becoming one technological safeguard on which regulators are focusing. As described earlier in this chapter, Massachusetts requires companies handling the personal information of its residents to encrypt such information when stored on portable devices and when transmitted over public networks or wirelessly. Nevada also adopted a similar law mandating encryption of personal information during electronic transmission and while in storage on data storage devices. Most other states exempt companies from data breach notification obligations if the exposed data is encrypted, but more states will likely implement encryption requirements of their own. Indeed, the California Attorney General recently issued a report finding that roughly 1.4 million Californians would not have had their personal information put at risk if companies had encrypted sensitive data and stating that California will make investigating breaches of unencrypted data a top priority going forward.

Addressing Security Breaches

One of the best strategies to manage a data security breach is to be prepared. Data breaches require companies to act quickly to mitigate potential harm and to comply with the myriad of federal and state breach notification obligations. Thus, before any breach occurs, companies should first conduct internal reviews and risk assessments to identify the weaknesses in their security measures where potential breaches are likely to occur. Common weaknesses include lax password and physical security measures, unsecured laptops and portable devices, and improper disposal of sensitive data. Companies should then take steps to reduce any risks identified in an internal review, such as by implementing appropriate technical safeguards and revising internal policies and protocols, as well as conduct ongoing risk management to identify developing risks. It is important for companies to be proactive and take appropriate measures to prevent breaches before they occur. Companies should monitor their security measures for relevant risks and assess their information security programs for potential shortcomings. Companies also should ensure that service provider agreements adequately address breach notification and response obligations. In addition, companies need to be cognizant that breaches can occur at any point in the chain of custody of personal information.

Companies that handle personal information also should ensure that they have an incident response plan in place before any breach occurs. The plan should outline the steps companies should take to respond, including investigating the extent of the breach and notifying affected customers and relevant law enforcement. Companies also should designate a team responsible for managing breach response, including internal employees and outside counsel, and should train employees on how to identify and report potential breaches. Engaging outside counsel early in the game can assist in protecting the companies' response under the attorney-client privilege and work product doctrine. Having a crisis management firm or internal team at the ready in case of a large-scale breach will save you critical response time should the worst occur. Ultimately, however, the scope of the response plan should reflect the size and complexity of the company as well as the sensitivity of the personal information involved.

Once a breach has occurred, companies need to act quickly to contain the breach and mitigate any potential harm. Companies need to accurately identify the scope and nature of the breach. Companies should involve their internal and external legal teams immediately, and if necessary, a forensic team that can investigate the breach under the cloak of the attorney-client privilege. Companies will then need to evaluate their notification obligations under the various state and federal breach notification laws. Companies should then take remedial steps to shore up the weaknesses that caused the breach, including identifying and addressing security gaps, ensuring existing policies are adequate in light of the breach, and conducting additional staff training to prevent future breaches.

Data breaches can be extremely costly. The Ponemon Institute recently published a study finding that the average total organizational cost of data breaches in the United States was almost $5.5 million. The study also found that the healthcare and financial services industries suffered the most on a per capita basis as the result of data breaches. The costs companies incur come from various sources. Fines and penalties issued by regulators can be the most significant costs of data breaches, ranging into the millions of dollars, in addition to legal costs related to regulatory investigations. Companies also incur significant costs from the numerous actions needed to adequately respond to breaches, including customer notification, forensic investigations, and credit monitoring for affected individuals. There is also a host of collateral losses associated with bad publicity and the loss of goodwill. The Ponemon report, though, demonstrated that companies can benefit from sizeable cost savings by having a strong security posture, having an incident response plan in place, and engaging consultants to help mitigate breach harm.

Top Privacy, Data Security, and Surveillance Challenges

Social Media

One issue that will remain a topic of debate in the privacy community relates to social media. The rise of platforms such as Facebook and Twitter present unique challenges for businesses across all industries. One major issue companies face is the disclosure of confidential or sensitive information via social media by employees. In particular, companies in heavily regulated industries, such as the financial and medical sectors, need to pay extra attention to the risks of social media. Companies should implement social media policies that plainly outline appropriate uses of such platforms. Companies also need to be aware of developments in legislation and regulation related to social media. For example, some states have passed, and many more are considering, laws prohibiting employers from asking current and prospective employees for their social media account information.

Mobile Device Data Collection

The privacy concerns related to mobile device data collection are another key area to address. Mobile technology has advanced significantly in recent years, and consequently, so too have methods for collecting and mining personal information. This year, the FTC issued a report addressing the major privacy issues related to mobile devices and recommending ways the mobile marketplace can better inform consumers and protect personal information. Moreover, the FTC recently settled charges against HTC related to HTC's alleged failure to take reasonable measures to secure the software for its smartphones and tablet computers, placing sensitive information about millions of consumers at risk. Viewed as a sign of the increased scrutiny to come, we anticipate that the regulatory environment surrounding mobile devices will become much more onerous in the near future.

There are also important data security concerns that companies need to take into account as the workplace integrates developing remote access and telecommuting platforms. As described earlier in this chapter, Massachusetts has strict requirements for the encryption of portable devices containing personal information; these regulations are likely just the tip of the spear.

Surveillance Concerns

There also will likely be major developments in US law regarding surveillance. One significant piece of proposed legislation would update the ECPA, which was enacted in 1986 and has been largely criticized as being outdated. The proposed bill would require authorities to obtain a search warrant to access e-mail stored online. Currently, the ECPA allows law enforcement to compel disclosure of e-mail stored longer than 180 days through subpoenas rather than warrants. Moreover, in response to the revelation of the National Security Agency's electronic data collection programs, Congress may likely pass legislation narrowing the government's ability to mine information stored by Internet service and cloud computing providers. In fact, Senator Patrick Leahy recently introduced the FISA Accountability and Privacy Protection Act, which would require the government to show that the records it seeks are relevant to an authorized investigation linked to a foreign agent or group.

In addition, lawmakers are showing increased interest in geolocation privacy legislation. Bills have been introduced in Congress that would not only restrict the government's ability to track location information, but would also require companies collecting location information about individuals to obtain prior opt-in consent.

Conclusion

Privacy issues will continue to arise as technology and data collection advance. For the most part though, privacy laws have had difficulty tackling the increasing collection and use of personal information. Lawmakers likely will try to shore up shortcomings in the privacy laws to address emerging concerns, and regulators charged with enforcing the various federal and state privacy laws will more closely scrutinize company information security practices. Companies generally are now more aware of, and sensitive to, privacy implications and issues. Nevertheless, privacy practitioners will still play a major role in guiding companies through the myriad of existing and impending laws, regulations, and best practices that police the privacy and data security landscape.

Key Takeaways

- The Gramm-Leach-Bliley Act set forth an important data security standard: Information security programs must be tailored to each company's risks, size, and the scope of their information collection and use practices. This "one size does not fit all" approach remains a cornerstone of data security across all businesses.
- One significant challenge companies face is that cloud providers typically offer standard form agreements that provide basic and minimum data security protections. Companies should consult with their attorneys in negotiating these agreements to better protect information in the cloud. In particular, companies should be wary of contracts from vendors that offer vague assurances of "reasonable" security.
- Smaller entities with reduced IT capabilities, including small businesses and non-profits, have struggled with the increased costs and obligations associated with compliance with the state. Outside counsel with experience and expertise in state laws and with developing information security policies are an invaluable resource for entities seeking to attain compliance.
- Companies should take a three-prong approach to data management and data security: assessment and investigation, risk management, and compliance monitoring.
- All companies that handle personal information should have an incident response plan in place before any breach occurs. The plan should outline the steps companies should take to respond, including investigating the extent of the breach and notifying affected customers and relevant law enforcement.

Brenda R. Sharton, a partner with Goodwin Proctor LLP, is a veteran litigator with more than twenty-three years of experience. Ms. Sharton is a member of the Executive Committee and also Chairs the firm's Business Litigation practice as well as the firm's Privacy & Data Security Practice.

Ms. Sharton advises and represents corporations, senior executives, boards of directors in complex commercial and business litigation matters, internal investigations, and civil regulatory matters.

In addition to business litigation, she focuses her practice on data privacy breach investigations and litigation, having defended numerous class actions related to the use of flash cookies as well as malware and other breach types. Ms. Sharton also was recently lead trial counsel for a financial services company in a landmark case that involved an alleged breach of the bank's online security system through keylogging malware. The case is one of the first of its kind in the nation and was named a "national case to watch" by American Banker.

Ms. Sharton has been recognized by Legal 500 US *for her financial services and privacy litigation work and for the past five consecutive years has been named in* Boston *magazine as a "Massachusetts Super Lawyer" in the area of business litigation.*

Acknowledgment: *The author would like to acknowledge the valuable assistance of Goodwin Procter LLP associate, Scott J. Carpenter.*

The Transformation of the "Right to Privacy" and Its Unintended Liability Consequences

Michael O'Neil

Partner

DLA Piper LLP

ASPATORE

Introduction

The explosion in the collection, use, and disclosure of consumer information by businesses, particularly in the Internet and mobile application industries, has put the ambiguous concept of the "right of privacy" front and center in the nation's dialogue. The ambiguity of the personal right is due, in part, to its uncertain origin. The concept is grounded neither in the US Constitution nor the common law. Even when the "right of privacy" was first codified as common law torts, the claimed right was more conceptual than tangible.

More recently, federal and state legislation over the last four decades has transformed the uncertain "right of privacy." Separate legislation now regulates the use and disclosure of specific consumer information in a variety of contexts. Going further, much of that legislation creates express rights to sue and permitted (or mandated) the recovery of liquidated damages, as well as attorney's fees and punitive damages. As a result, a conceptual right to privacy originating from the desire to compensate for the obvious emotional harm resulting from public disclosure of private facts is now the basis for awarding thousands of dollars to a successful plaintiff, even if no harm resulted from the challenged conduct. The litigation liability threat is exponentially multiplied by court rules allowing such claims to be prosecuted on behalf of a class, and the courts' increasing willingness to permit such statutory "privacy" claims to proceed on behalf of a class. The result, as courts routinely acknowledge, is the threat of a class award for statutory damages for violations of law that cause no real harm. By multiplying the individual recovery mandated by statute by the number of class members, the bankruptcy of a defendant company is often threatened.

Legislation governing the use and disclosure of consumer information is certain to become more common. However, at the same time, we must reassess the largely unintended consequences of such legislation and their generous remedial schemes. Providing an individual the right to recover compensatory damages for emotional distress suffered, for example, by being surreptitiously videotaped in a gym locker room may be a reasonable, if not laudable, goal. The privacy invasion, and the resulting harm, is clear. However, the "right to privacy" does not always support the collective class right to recover millions of dollars in statutory damages for prohibited disclosures of information, e.g., the printing of a credit account expiration date on a receipt, which causes no harm.

This chapter examines the laws, court rules, and judicial decisions that, taken together, often result in threatened massive liability for violations of so-called "privacy" legislation that do not implicate the premise for the "right to privacy."

The Common Law "Right to Privacy"

Legal concepts such as ownership interests in real property and judicial enforcement of contract rights originated centuries ago in English common law and are now well-established in the United States. The "right of privacy," in comparison, is a relatively new concept, borne out of business and technological changes, which continues to evolve. The US Constitution makes no reference to a right to privacy, and less than a handful of state constitutions do so. It is commonly accepted that the genesis of today's right to privacy was the 1890 article by Samuel Warren and Louis Brandeis "The Right to Privacy."[1] The authors were the first to argue for judicial recognition of the right "to be left alone," premised upon then-existing common law personal rights and "[r]ecent inventions and business methods [that] call attention to the next step which must be taken for the protection of the person."[2]

The right to privacy moved beyond the conceptual stage when William Prosser organized the nascent theory into four categories.[3] Prosser later codified in the Restatement (Second) of Torts the four common law privacy torts:

1. Unreasonable intrusion upon another's seclusion or solitude, or into his private affairs;
2. Public disclosure of embarrassing private facts;
3. Publicity which places the plaintiff in a false light in the public eye; and
4. Appropriation of a person's name or likeness for advantage.[4]

[1] Samuel Warren & Louis D. Brandeis, *The Right to Privacy*, 4 HARV. L. R. 193 (1890).
[2] *Id.* at 195.
[3] William Prosser, *Privacy*, 48 CALIF. L. REV. 383 (1960).
[4] RESTATEMENT OF TORTS (Second), §§652A-652I (1977).

An element common to each of these four torts is the disclosure of private facts that causes emotional harm, e.g., the publication of information related to a person's income tax data, sexual relations, or medical treatment. Like other tortious conduct that does not directly result in monetary harm, e.g., libel, such torts can give rise to a compensatory award of damages and, in cases of egregious conduct, punitive damages. The particular award amount is highly fact-specific and determined by the judge or a jury. Just as injury caused by the defendant's conduct is a basic element of any tort claim, injury caused by the privacy intrusion is a basic element of common law privacy torts.

The basic injury element of tort law has also proved dispositive—and fatal—to lawsuits arising from data security breaches. Most states have enacted laws obligating businesses to alert consumers when their personal information has been the subject of a data security breach, e.g., the theft of a computer laptop or the hacking into of a website. Although such laws do not provide for a cause of action arising from such a data breach, class action lawsuits premised upon such security breaches have become commonplace in recent years.

Such breaches typically do not result in the misuse of the personal information or other harm to the affected consumer. For example, the data may remain encrypted and therefore practically undisclosed, or is otherwise insufficient to facilitate the credit card fraud or identity theft that the breach notice laws were intended to prevent. Therefore, lawsuits against companies experiencing a data breach typically assert common law claims premised upon other alleged injuries, i.e., the fear of future misuse of the data and the related cost of monitoring against such misuse. However, with few exceptions, such lawsuits typically are summarily dismissed by the courts for failure to allege a cognizable injury giving rise to a tort or breach of contract claim.[5]

Causes of Action and Recoveries Created by "Privacy" Legislation

Outside the context of the common law, however, Congress has eliminated the fundamental harm requirement by legislating against certain information

[5] *See, e.g.*, *Pisciotta v. Old Nat. Bancorp*, 499 F.3d 629, 640 (7th Cir. 2007) (affirming dismissal of negligence and breach of implied contract claims based on hacking of bank data for lack of cognizable harm). Other suits have been dismissed for failure to establish the federal jurisdictional requirement that the conduct give rise to a cognizable harm. *See*, e.g., *Reilly v. Ceridian Corp.*, 664 F.3d 38, 46 (3d Cir. 2011) (affirming dismissal for lack of Article III standing of negligence claims based on security breach of payroll data).

use and disclosure practices and creating specific remedies available when a prohibited practice occurs.

One of the earliest privacy statutes regulating the collection, disclosure and use of consumer information is the federal Fair Credit Reporting Act, (FCRA)[6] which was originally enacted in 1970 to regulate the credit reporting industry. In the preamble to the statute, Congress acknowledged the "vital role" in the banking system played by credit bureaus.[7] Balanced with the needs of the financial system, however, was the need for credit bureaus, or "consumer reporting agencies" (CRAs), to "exercise their grave responsibilities with fairness, impartiality, and a respect for the consumer's right to privacy."[8]

To achieve that balance, the FCRA created new rights of consumers with respect to credit bureaus and the information held by them and other CRAs. For example, the FCRA sets forth the only "permissible purposes" for the delivery and use of "consumer reports." The FCRA also created a consumer's right to obtain copies of their information from CRAs and to dispute any inaccurate information. The CRA must then investigate the disputed information and provide the consumer with the results of the investigation.

Liquidated damages without proof of harm

Along with these and other new rights, the FCRA created causes of action for violation of "any" of the statute's provisions.[9] As originally enacted, a consumer who could prove a violation of any of the statute's requirements was entitled to recover "any actual damages," plus costs and reasonable attorney's fees.[10] Proof of a "willful" violation also allowed the court to award punitive damages.[11]

In 1996, however, the FCRA was amended to enlarge the recovery allowed where a violation of "any" requirement of the FCRA was deemed "willful." In

---

[6] 15 U.S.C. §§ 1681 *et seq.* (West).
[7] 15 U.S.C. § 1681(a)(3).
[8] 15 U.S.C. § 1681(a)(4).
[9] 15 U.S.C. §§ 1681n(a), 1681o(a).
[10] 15 U.S.C. § 1681n(a).
[11] 15 U.S.C. § 1681n(a)(2).

that instance, as an alternative to recovery of "actual damages," a successful plaintiff could recover statutory damages ranging from $100 to $1,000.[12]

Later court decisions interpreting the FCRA transformed the impact of the amendment allowing consumers to recover statutory damages. Most notably, some courts have held (without much explanation) that proof of an actual injury caused by a violation of the statute is not required to recover statutory damages of $100 to $1,000, plus costs and attorney's fees.[13] Separately, the requisite proof that a willful violation of the FCRA has occurred has been reduced. The US Supreme Court held that a finding that a violation of the FCRA was more than simply "negligent," § 1681o(a), but "willful," § 1681n(a), can be premised upon not only knowing or intentional conduct, but also upon merely reckless conduct.[14] The Supreme Court strived, but failed, to articulate a precise definition of the distinction between negligence and recklessness.[15] Thus, under the FCRA, a consumer who suffered no harm due to a reckless violation of the complex statute nonetheless can recover statutory damages of up to $1,000, in addition to attorney's fees and punitive damages.

Other federal consumer privacy statutes similarly restrict the use and disclosure of information and permit the recovery of statutory damages, without requiring any proof of harm, for violations of those prohibitions.[16] For example, the Drivers' Privacy Protection Act restricts the use and disclosure of consumer information contained in state motor vehicle records.[17] A person who obtains, discloses, or uses a consumer's personal information in a knowing violation of the statute can be liable to that individual for $2,500 in "liquidated damages," punitive damages, plus costs

---

[12] Pub. L. No. 104-208, § 2412(b), 110 Stat. 3009-446 (codified as amended at 15 U.S.C. § 1681n(1)(A) (1996)).

[13] *See, e.g., Murray v. GMAC Mortgage Corp.*, 434 F.3d 948, 953 (7th Cir. 2006).

[14] *Safeco Ins. Co. of Am. v. Burr*, 551 U.S. 47 (2007).

[15] *Id.* at 68-69. The Court explained that "a company subject to (the) FCRA does not act in reckless disregard of it unless the action is not only a violation under a reasonable reading of the statute's terms, but shows that the company ran a risk of violating the law substantially greater than the risk associated with a reading that was merely careless." *Id.* (internal citations and footnote omitted).

[16] The constitutionality of governmental restrictions on the accurate communication of speech has been questioned, e.g., *Trans Union Corp. v. F.T.C.*, 81 F.3d 228, 235 (D.C. Cir. 1996). However, the First Amendment issue is beyond the scope of this chapter.

[17] 18 U.S.C. §§ 2721-25 (West).

and attorney's fees.[18] Similarly, the Telephone Consumer Protection Act generally prohibits unsolicited telemarketing calls and faxes, as well as text messages and autodialed calls to cellular phones without the consumer's consent.[19] The statute provides for a minimum recovery of $500 per violation, and allows up to $1,500 for a willful or knowing violation.[20] The Wiretap Act[21] generally prohibits the interception, disclosure, or use of wire and electronic communications by an "electronic communications service" (such as an e-mail provider or social networking site), and allows for the recovery of statutory damages of $10,000, or $100 per day, whichever is greater.[22] Similarly, the Stored Communications Act generally prohibits electronic communications services from divulging stored communications to an unintended recipient, and also prevents unauthorized access to stored electronic communications.[23] The statute allows a minimum recovery of $1,000 for knowing or intentional violations of the statute, and similarly to the other consumer privacy statutes, and does so even in the absence of any actual harm.[24] [25]

Elimination of constitutional harm requirement

Such consumer privacy legislation not only creates the right to sue in the absence of harm, but also serves in effect to eliminate constitution-based jurisdictional requirements that a federal court plaintiff must allege some cognizable harm. Article III of the US Constitution has been read as requiring that a plaintiff have "standing" to maintain a lawsuit in federal court. A key component of such standing is that the plaintiff must allege an "injury-in-fact" caused by the defendant's conduct.[26] Therefore, for example, the US Supreme Court has held that someone complaining of

---

[18] 18 U.S.C. § 2724 (1997).
[19] 47 U.S.C. § 227 (2010).
[20] 47 U.S.C. § 227(b)(3).
[21] 18 U.S.C. §§ 2510-22 (West).
[22] 18 U.S.C. § 2520(c)(2).
[23] 18 U.S.C. §§ 2701-12 (West).
[24] 18 U.S.C. § 2707 (2002).
[25] The states have also enacted consumer privacy laws that allow for the recovery of statutory damages without proof of harm. *See, e.g.*, Michigan Video Rental Privacy Act, Mich. Comp. Laws Ann. §§ 445.1711-15 (allowing recovery, in lieu of actual damages, of $5,000, plus costs and attorney's fees, for disclosure of records reflecting the purchase of a book or sound or video recording).
[26] *Lujan v. Defenders of Wildlife*, 504 U.S. 555, 560 (1992).

constitutional violations cannot bring suit if they cannot show a personal injury from the alleged violation.[27]

Given the well-established principle of standing, a plaintiff asserting a violation of a federal privacy statute that resulted in no harm should be precluded from suing in federal court. However, courts have held that where Congress creates a statutory right and a corresponding cause of action for a violation of the statute, the Article III injury-in-fact requirement is met by the simple allegation that the statute has been violated, even when there is no resulting harm to the plaintiff.[28] In *Edwards v. First American Corp.*, for example, the plaintiff on behalf of a class alleged that an exclusive referral arrangement between her title insurance provider and her settlement agent violated the federal Real Estate Settlement Procedures Act. Even though there was no risk that the alleged violation harmed the class, e.g., by causing them to pay higher fees, the lawsuit sought the statutory remedy of "an amount equal to three times the amount of any charge paid for such settlement service."[29] The Ninth Circuit affirmed the district court ruling that Congress' mere creation of a statutory cause of action established the plaintiff's Article III standing.

When the US Supreme Court agreed to hear an appeal from the *Edwards* ruling in 2011, there was optimism that the Court would reaffirm the injury-in-fact requirement, and clarify that Congress could not manufacture Article III standing by prohibiting a practice and then creating a concomitant right to sue. As the Supreme Court had previously held: "[T]he requirement of injury in fact is a hard floor of Article III jurisdiction that cannot be removed by statute."[30] However, seven months after hearing arguments in the *Edwards* case, and on the last day of that Court's term, the Court without explanation dismissed its writ of certiorari "as improvidently granted."[31] Thus, the Supreme Court avoided deciding whether the constitutional injury-in-fact requirement would fill the gap created by federal statutes that allow an award of liquidated damages without proof of harm.

---

[27] *Valley Forge Christian Coll. v. Americans United for Separation of Church & State, Inc.*, 454 U.S. 464, 485 (1982).
[28] *Edwards v. First Am. Corp.*, 610 F.3d 514, 517 (9th Cir. 2010).
[29] 12 U.S.C. § 2607(d)(2) (2011).
[30] *Summers v. Earth Island Inst.*, 555 U.S. 488, 497 (2009).
[31] *First Am. Fin. Corp. v. Edwards*, 132 S. Ct. 2536 (2012).

The Impact of Class Certification under Federal Rule 23

The impact of federal statutes that allow the award of statutory damages for violations that cause no harm is exponentially multiplied by the class-action mechanism of Federal Rule of Civil Procedure 23.[32]

As their name suggests, the Federal Rules of Civil Procedure set forth the processes for civil litigation in US federal district courts. The eighty-six rules and their subparts address a wide range of topics, e.g., the filing of the initial complaint, the exchange of information and documents as part of the discovery process, trial, and judgments. Federal statute requires, however, that the rules must address only procedure. "Such rules shall not abridge, enlarge, or modify any substantive rights."[33]

Federal Rule 23 empowers district courts to certify that claims can be asserted on behalf of unnamed persons, i.e., a class action. The Rule sets forth the requirements that a plaintiff and plaintiff's counsel must satisfy to proceed as a class action.[34] For claims seeking primarily monetary damages, special rules apply; the court must find that common questions of law or fact predominate over individualized issues and that a class action is superior to other available litigation methods.[35] Given the preclusive effect of a class action on unnamed class members, and the requirements of due process, the Rule also establishes requirements for notifying class members of the litigation, its impact on their rights, and their options.[36] The Rule also describes a court's duties in connection with approving a proposed class settlement.[37] Relatedly, the rule authorizes courts to "award reasonable attorney's fees and nontaxable costs that are authorized by law or by the parties' agreement."[38]

Statutory Privacy Claims are Routinely Certified as Class Claims

Statutory damages claims for violation of federal and state privacy laws are ripe for class certification treatment. Such claims are often premised upon the

---

[32] FED. R. CIV. P. 23.

[33] 28 U.S.C. § 2072(b). Notably, the court rules are issued by the US Supreme Court and become effective without any action by Congress. *See* 28 U.S.C. 2074 (West).

[34] FED. R. CIV. P. 23(a), (b).

[35] FED. R. CIV. P. 23(b)(3).

[36] FED. R. CIV. P. 23(c).

[37] FED. R. CIV. P. 23(e).

[38] FED. R. CIV. P. 23(h).

requisite common facts, i.e., a company's uniform business practice regarding the use or disclosure of consumer information. As noted *supra*, such claims are often premised upon statutes that provide for a minimum recovery of statutory damages without requiring proof of harm caused by the defendant's practices. Therefore, the "individualized issues" of establishing that each class member was harmed by the conduct, and determining the appropriate amount of damages for each class member, are not present.

Some courts have declined to certify certain claims for class treatment due to the possible "annihilating effect" of a class judgment against a defendant.[39] Rule 23(b)(3) requires that, when certifying a class for claims seeking money damages, the district court determine "that a class action is superior to other available methods" of litigating the claim. Courts have found such superiority absent when a successful class action might result in a massive statutory damages award that is disproportionate to any harm suffered by the class, and/or threatens to bankrupt the defendant.

District courts considering FCRA statutory damages claims based on credit card receipts that violated the statute often refused to certify classes due to the enormous liability disproportionate to any harm. One example is *Bateman v. Am. Multi-Cinema, Inc.*, where the defendant was charged with violating the FCRA, by including more than the last five digits of the credit account number on the receipts provided to movie ticket purchasers.[40] On behalf of himself and other consumers who received such receipts, the plaintiff sought to recover statutory damages of $100-$1,000 for each willful violation. Because 290,000 violative receipts were issued during the class period, the cinema's potential liability was $29 million to $290 million. The district court found this amount enormous and out of proportion to any harm suffered by the class, and denied class certification on the grounds that the class was not the superior method of litigating such claims. On appeal, and distinguishing that court's prior case law, the Ninth Circuit reversed.[41] The appellate court examined the Fair and Accurate Credit

[39] *See e.g., Castano v. Am. Tobacco Co.*, 84 F.3d 734, 746 (5th Cir. 1996) (reversing certification of a mass tort class action due to the specter of "significantly higher damage awards" and "insurmountable pressure" to settle); *Ratner v. Chem. Bank New York Trust Co.*, 54 F.R.D. 412, 413 (S.D.N.Y. 1972) (declining to certify a claim for statutory damages under the Truth In Lending Act for failure to disclose an interest rate where no actual damages were suffered).

[40] 15 U.S.C. § 1681c(g) (West).

[41] *Bateman v. Am. Multi-Cinema, Inc.*, 623 F.3d 708 (9th Cir. 2010).

Transactions Act (FACTA) and congressional silence on the issue of class relief, in determining that the proportionality of the damages to the harm suffered is "an irrelevant consideration."[42]

Federal courts have rejected the rationale in the context of other FCRA claims, holding that the possibility of a "ruinously high" statutory damages award was not an appropriate consideration in determining whether to certify a class under Rule 23. In *Murray v. GMAC Mortgage Corp.*, the plaintiff sued, on behalf of a class, a potential creditor that had accessed her credit history in alleged violation of the FCRA. The district court refused to certify a class, in part, because "[i]f Murray and the proposed class members were to prevail at trial, GMAC would face potential liability in the billions of dollars for purely technical violations of the FCRA... Rule 23 is not intended to encourage such abuses of the class action mechanism."[43] The appellate court reversed, holding that it was not Rule 23, but "the legislative decision to authorize awards as high as $1,000 per person" and the defendant's uniform business practices affecting more than a million persons, which created the risk of substantial damages. The appellate court also noted that, unlike other federal consumer protection statutes, the FCRA does not contain a cap on the total recovery in a class action.[44] For example, the Fair Debt Collection Practices Act limits total recovery in a class action to "the lesser of $500,000 or 1 per centum of the net worth of the debt collector."[45] Notably, the appellate court in *Murray* mused that the existence of class action lawsuits threatening significant liability for purely technical violations of the federal statute might "lead Congress to amend the Fair Credit Reporting Act; maybe not."[46] To date, Congress has not accepted this invitation from the courts.

The appellate court in *Murray* grudgingly noted the risk that a statutory damage class award may be "unconstitutionally excessive." The court, however, instructed that "constitutional limits are best applied after a class has been certified."[47]

---

[42] *Id.* at 721.

[43] *Murray v. GMAC Mortgage Corp.*, 434 F.3d 948, 953 (7th Cir. 2006).

[44] *Id.*

[45] 15 U.S.C. § 1692k(a)(2)(B)(ii) (West).

[46] *Murray*, 434 F.3d at 954.

[47] *Id.* (citing *State Farm Mut. Auto. Ins. Co. v. Campbell*, 538 U.S. 408 (2003)). Although beyond the scope of this chapter, which examines privacy legislation within the principles underlying the "right to privacy," the very real due process concerns arising from a class award

Statutory Damages Class Actions Threaten "Settlement Blackmail"

Lawsuits seeking statutory damages under the FCRA and other federal privacy statutes are popular among plaintiff's class action lawyers. Because a claim can be premised upon the violation of "any" of the many requirements of the FCRA, numerous factual circumstances can give rise to a possible claim. As noted *supra*, there are fewer obstacles to obtaining class certification of claims asserting statutory damages rather than actual damages premised upon individualized circumstances. Of course, the guaranteed award of attorney's fees for the successful prosecution of any FCRA violation, negligent or willful, is also attractive. All these circumstances create a greater likelihood that such claims will be settled before the plaintiff's lawyer must prove the case in a courtroom.

Class action settlements often involve the defendant(s) paying amounts into a "common fund," in exchange for a release of liability from all class members. The cost of notice to the class, settlement administrative costs, and attorney's fees payable to plaintiff's counsel, are paid from the "common fund." Amounts remaining in the fund after such payments are distributed to class members, typically only those who affirmatively register for such distribution. It is not uncommon for only a fraction of eligible class members, i.e., 5 percent to 10 percent to seek recovery from the class settlement. However, because fees are generally calculated as a percentage of the total common fund, plaintiff's counsel are incentivized to insist upon large class settlements, even if not necessary, to fairly compensate class members who feel aggrieved by the defendant's conduct.

Federal courts have long noted the coercive effect of class actions on defendants who are forced to settle rather than litigate a bet-the-company lawsuit. As Judge Posner of the Seventh Circuit Court of Appeals noted, the well-respected Second Circuit jurist Judge Friendly called settlements induced by a small probability of an immense judgment in a class action "blackmail settlements."[48] In recognition of the settlement pressure created by class certification, Rule 23 was amended in 1998 to allow permissive interlocutory appeals of decisions granting or denying class certification. Rule 23(f). Before that amendment, a defendant faced with an unfavorable

of statutory damages also demand re-examination of the practical impact of such laws.

[48] *Matter of Rhone-Poulenc Rorer, Inc.*, 51 F.3d 1293, 1298-1300 (7th Cir. 1995).

class certification decision was required to litigate the class claims to judgment before being able to appeal. However, such petitions to appeal class certification rulings are more often than not denied.

The Unintended Consequences of Privacy Statutes and Their Remedied Schemes

The combination of (a) the statutory damages remedial schemes of many federal privacy law and (b) Rule 23 creates the risk of a significant classwide damages judgment for what may be technical violations of the law that caused no real privacy harm. Even where a credible privacy interest has been impaired, the remedial schemes impose sanctions far beyond those commensurate with that privacy violation.

Perhaps the most familiar example of the unintended consequences arising from class certification of claims for statutory damages under consumer privacy statutes is the onslaught of litigation arising from the credit card receipt provisions of the FCRA. By the Fair and Accurate Credit Transactions Act of 2003 (FACTA), Congress amended the FCRA to add numerous provisions intended to combat identity theft, thereby expanding the statute's scope beyond its original focus on compiled information used to make credit, insurance, and other eligibility decisions.[49] One such amendment required merchants to truncate the account number printed on credit and debit card receipts provided to the consumer, and display no more than the last five digits of the number.[50]

Even before passage of the FACTA amendments to the FCRA, truncation of account numbers had been the industry standard. However, most retail industries were (initially) unaware that FACTA also prohibited the display of an account expiration date on a receipt. Not so with the plaintiffs' class action bar. Immediately after the FACTA credit card receipt provision became effective, hundreds of class action lawsuits were filed, against both large, national retailers and smaller, local merchants. Seizing upon the pre-existing remedial provisions of the FCRA, putative class plaintiffs alleged "willful" FCRA violations based upon receipts that did not mask the account expiration date, and sought $100 to $1,000 in

---

[49] Pub. L. No. 108-159, 117 Stat. 1952.

[50] 15 U.S.C. § 1681c(g) (West).

statutory damages for each printed receipt. Such lawsuits did not and could not allege any harm to consumers resulting from the printing of expiration dates. Nevertheless, a number of federal courts certified FACTA receipt claims as class actions and denied defendants' motions for summary judgment. The litigation threatened a broad range of companies with liability that would only bring bankruptcy.

In a rare example of quick action, Congress stepped in to erase the unintended consequences of its earlier legislation. While most FCRA receipt cases remained pending, Congress passed the Credit and Debit Card Receipt Clarification Act of 2007,[51] without a single dissenting vote. Intended to address the hundreds of class actions and crushing damages faced by large and small business, Congress "clarified" that it was not a "willful" violation of the FCRA to print an expiration date on a receipt that properly truncates the credit card account number.[52] The express basis for the legislation was a Congressional finding that the lawsuits did not allege any risk of identity theft (the original legislative concern). Congress also accepted industry expert opinion that truncation of the account number, even with the display of the expiration date, was sufficient to permit identity theft. By its unanimous passage of the Clarification Act, Congress acknowledged, and remedied, the unintended consequences of this FACTA amendment.

Of course, the duties of a merchant printing credit card receipts are only one set of the numerous obligations imposed by the FCRA. Congress has made no effort to modify the impact of the statute's remedies when other obligations are not met, but creating no real harm to consumers.

Proposed Solutions

Therefore, how can the unintended consequences of the remedial schemes of federal privacy legislation, coupled with class action treatment, be ameliorated?

The most appropriate fix is a legislative one. Putting aside (for the moment) First Amendment and due process issues, and the economic impact of

[51] Pub. L No. 110–241, 122 Stat 1565 (2008).

[52] Given the widespread publicity given to the hundreds of FACTA lawsuits filed shortly after the Act's effective date, the clarification applied only to receipts printed before the Act's effective date, thereby allowing suits for future violations.

restrictions on disclosures of accurate information, legislative bans on the use and disclosure of certain information in certain contexts may continue to be appropriate, and consistent with basic principles of individual privacy. However, Congress must be more cognizant of the consequence of establishing a right to sue and guaranteed recoveries, regardless of whether the plaintiff suffered any harm. Even if statutory damages are eliminated, providing for an award of attorney's fees and punitive damages where a privacy statute is violated sufficiently incentivizes a plaintiff—and his or her counsel—to sue when the claimant is aggrieved (or offended) by a particular business practice. Even if an award of statutory damages is viewed as also necessary to incentivize the prosecution of such laws, Congress must contemplate the impact of such claims when brought on behalf of a class of thousands, if not millions, of people.

Like other consumer protection statutes that provide for statutory damage, e.g., the Fair Debt Collection Practice Act, privacy legislation creating a right to sue should address the recoveries available in a class action.[53] The federal "privacy" legislation referenced in this chapter does not provide or otherwise address the availability and extent of class remedies. Congress should amend such laws to place a cap on total class liability, e.g., a lump-sum amount or a percentage of a company's net worth. Alternatively, Congress should make statutory damages unavailable in a class action; or Congress should condition the recovery of classwide statutory damages on evidence of real classwide harm.

As contributors of a sort to the current quagmire, the judiciary can also play a role in mitigating the unintended consequences of privacy class action claims. Judges should not abdicate the discretion afforded to them under Rule 23 to determine that class treatment of a claim is not "superior to other available methods" for adjudication of the claims. Congressional silence on the application of a statute's remedial scheme to a class action cannot be read, as some courts have, as a legislative directive to allow such recoveries by a class. In any event, it is in the judicial context of specific facts and the mathematics of a possible annihilating class statutory damages award, that a court must determine whether class certification is inappropriate.

[53] 15 U.S.C. §§ 1692-1692p (West).

More broadly, Congress, the courts, and the public at large must reexamine notions of privacy and its role in society today. Unlike the privacy intrusions that spurred creation of the "right to privacy," many of the business practices that may run afoul of "privacy" legislation cause no real privacy intrusion. Indeed, such practices (unlike those targeted over a century ago) have some societal benefit. It is beyond dispute that there are fundamental differences between being unknowingly videotaped in a locker room shower and the disclosure of a credit card expiration date on a receipt. Even if there is logic to prohibiting the latter practice, there is no logic to exposing a company that unwittingly prints the expiration date to significant and perhaps bankrupting liability despite the absence of harm.

Conclusion

Invoking the "right to privacy," Congress and state legislatures have enacted prohibitions or other restrictions on the use and disclosure of consumer information. The legislation often creates a right to sue and provides for a minimum guaranteed individual recovery for a successful plaintiff and an award of fees for his or her attorney. Because such claims often can be brought even where the statutory violation caused no harm, they are ripe for class treatment, thereby multiplying exponentially the liability risk. As a result, companies are subject to significant, and sometimes annihilating, class judgments for a technical violation of a statute that causes no injury. Even before a class judgment is obtained, the threat of class liability can coerce a defendant to agree to a "blackmail settlement."

Some statutory provisions, e.g., restrictions on the permitted use of credit reports, serve the goal of consumer informational privacy. Other laws, e.g., the ban on displaying a credit card expiration date on the receipt provided to the consumer, do not. An award of statutory damages and attorneys' fees may serve the legitimate goal of incentivizing an individual to sue for a privacy invasion that causes some tangible harm. However, there is no reason to believe that Congress intended to create the specter of ruinous class liability for violations of law that caused no harm. Congress must be more cognizant of the consequences of a statutory damages remedy in the context of a class action. Separately, courts should decline to certify for class treatment "privacy" claims that allege no harm but risk a defendant's bankruptcy.

Key Takeaways

- All business using or even maintaining any kind of consumer information should become familiar with laws governing such data, and should monitor new legislation.
- Particular attention should be paid to laws that allow for private enforcement and incentivize lawsuits with guaranteed minimum recoveries and an award of attorney's fees.
- Litigators defending statutory "privacy" claims should continue to argue that class treatment of such claims that cause no harm but threaten minimum recoveries per class member are not "superior to other available methods" of adjudication, as required by Federal Rule 23.
- Legislators determined to enact further restrictions on the use of consumer information must ensure that the consequences of violating such laws are commensurate with the harm resulting from the violation.

Michael O'Neil, a partner with DLA Piper LLP, has concentrated his practice in the defense of class action privacy claims and has tried jury and bench trials in both state and federal courts. For more than twenty years, Mr. O'Neil has successfully defended against asserted class claims brought under the federal Fair Credit Reporting Act (FCRA), and its attendant threat of statutory damages.

Mr. O'Neil has represented a wide array of data furnishers in matters involving various types of sensitive consumer information, such as credit reports, criminal record information, and insurance support organizations and medical information. Mr. O'Neil has also represented a broad variety of defendants, e.g., Internet service providers, cellular phone companies, and retailers in class action and commercial litigation involving phone records, credit scores, and other large amounts of electronic data. Mr. O'Neil's practice also includes counseling clients regarding compliance with a wide spectrum of state and federal laws governing the use and disclosure of consumer financial, health, and other information and related regulations.

Acknowledgment: *The author would like to acknowledge the assistance of Albert Hartmann, an attorney in the Chicago office of DLA Piper LLP.*

Private Data Security Breach Litigation in the United States

Douglas H. Meal

Partner

Ropes & Gray LLP

ASPATORE

Introduction

As then-Federal Bureau of Investigation (FBI) Director Robert Mueller recently put it, "[T]here are only two types of companies: those that have been hacked and those that will be."[1] In recent years, more and more corporations have disclosed that they have been a victim of a data security breach, often as the result of sophisticated hackers (frequently in foreign countries) penetrating their computer systems and potentially stealing information about individuals such as the company's customers or employees.

Although data security breaches are now commonplace, those breaches where personal information is stolen or put at risk of being stolen often trigger legal claims by private plaintiffs seeking to characterize the breach as the result of unreasonable, lax measures by the breached company in protecting the personal information in question. In defending many data security breach victims against such claims, we have seen the range of contentions these plaintiffs make, and how courts have addressed them. As we explain below, such plaintiffs frequently struggle to plead and prove that the data security breach resulted from the victim's breach of its legal obligations, as opposed to an unfortunate perpetration of computer crime by third parties, and/or that any breach of legal obligations caused any recoverable injury.[2] As plaintiffs' lawyers continue to look for ways to overcome these difficulties, all data security practitioners should pay close attention to further developments in the case law and their implications for companies that collect or use information about individuals.

Potential Litigants against Companies that Have Suffered Data Security Breaches

Companies that suffer data security breaches can face claims by a wide variety of private litigants. The most common private litigant against a corporate victim of a data security breach is the individual or individuals, such as a

[1] *See* Prepared Remarks of Robert S. Mueller, Director, FBI, RSA Cyber Security Conference (Mar. 1, 2012), http://www.fbi.gov/news/speeches/combating-threats-in-the-cyber-world-outsmarting-terrorists-hackers-and-spies.

[2] We address here only claims by private parties. Victims of data security breaches can also face investigations or lawsuits by government agencies seeking to enforce consumer protection laws. We also focus here on data security breaches exposing information about individuals, as opposed to theft of trade secrets or other types of information exposure.

consumer or employee, whose data was allegedly stolen or may have been placed at risk of being stolen from the company during the breach.[3]

If payment card data was potentially stolen, the company may face claims not only by the cardholders whose card information was involved,[4] but also by the banks and credit unions that issued the cards, which seek compensation for the cost of reimbursing their customers for fraudulent charges, re-issuing cards, and monitoring compromised accounts.[5] Insurers who have reimbursed financial institutions for such losses may likewise seek to recover them from the breached company.[6] In addition, card brands such as Visa and MasterCard may impose fines for violating their rules governing data security practices and/or assessments to pay the financial institutions that issued the compromised cards for losses they claim to have incurred.[7]

A breached company may also face claims by other plaintiffs, including by shareholders under federal securities laws for allegedly inadequate disclosures of data security risks.[8]

Threshold Issues Relating to Injury and Damages

Private civil actions against companies that have suffered data security breaches raise a panoply of issues, but none more prevalent or decisive than those relating to injury and damages. This is because most plaintiffs in data

[3] *Bell v. Blizzard Entm't, Inc.*, No. 12-cv-09475, at *3 (C.D. Cal. July 11, 2013) (suit by consumers); *Reilly v. Ceridian Corp.*, 664 F.3d 38, 40 (3d Cir. 2011) (suit by employees).
[4] *Anderson v. Hannaford Bros. Co.*, 659 F.3d 151, 164 (1st Cir. 2011).
[5] *Lone Star Nat'l Bank, N.A. v. Heartland Payment Sys., Inc.*, 729 F.3d 421 (5th Cir. 2013); *In re TJX Companies Retail Sec. Breach Litig.*, 564 F.3d 489, 491-2 (1st Cir. 2009).
[6] *See Cumis Ins. Soc., Inc. v. Merrick Bank Corp.*, CIV07-374-TUC-CKJ, 2008 WL 4277877, at *1 (D. Ariz. Sept. 18, 2008).
[7] *See Genesco, Inc. v. Visa U.S.A. Inc.*, 3:13CV202, 2013 WL 3790647, at *1 (M.D. Tenn. July 18, 2013). In many instances, such as where the victim of the breach is a merchant, card brands such as Visa and MasterCard do not share a direct contractual relationship with the breached company. Instead, "acquiring banks" contract with Visa and MasterCard to become members of the payment card systems, and then these banks contract with merchants to sponsor their participation and enable them to accept card payments. Thus, when a merchant suffers a breach, the card brands generally impose fines and assessments directly on the acquiring banks, who then assert claims against their merchant customers for reimbursement. *Id.*
[8] *See, e.g., In re Heartland Payment Sys., Inc. Sec. Litig.*, CIV. 09–1043, 2009 WL 4798148, at *1-2 (D.N.J. Dec. 7, 2009).

security actions have not experienced any actual misuse or fraud resulting from the breach, but instead premise their claims on alternative theories of injury, such as the risk of harm. Judicial decisions addressing data security claims have placed clear limitations on the types of injuries the law will remedy. Further, even where there is injury sufficient to state a claim, a plaintiff also must show causation, including that the harm was the result of the particular breach at issue. With the widespread use of online storefronts, social media, and the countless other interactions in which consumers today share their information in the digital realm, and with the very frequency of breaches themselves, connecting any one incident of misuse to the specific breach at issue can prove challenging. Finally, otherwise recoverable damages may be foreclosed under principles specific to particular causes of action, such as the economic loss doctrine.

Added together, injury and damages issues account for a significant portion of the litigation that takes place in the data security space, and present plaintiffs with complex challenges that can prove difficult to overcome.

Cognizable Injury

Common to almost every cause of action plaintiffs assert against breached companies in the wake of a data breach, whether they be contractual, tortious, statutory, or equitable, is the essential element of cognizable injury.[9] With very few exceptions, a plaintiff must show that he or she suffered some appreciable, non-speculative, present harm to state a claim for relief.[10] So far, no element has proven more elusive for plaintiffs.[11] As explained below, absent allegations of actual, detrimental misuse of their information, plaintiffs have had great difficulty establishing any injury sufficient to support their claims.

Increased Risk of Future Harm: The most commonly alleged injury in data breach actions is an increased risk of future harm. Specifically, consumers frequently have alleged that as a result of the exposure of their information,

---

[9] *See, e.g., Shafran v. Harley-Davidson, Inc.*, No. 07 CIV. 01365 (GBD), 2008 WL 763177, at *2-3 (S.D.N.Y. Mar. 20, 2008).

[10] *See, e.g., Krottner v. Starbucks Corp.*, 406 F. App'x 129, 131 (9th Cir. 2010).

[11] As we explain below in the section on procedural issues, this lack of injury also often prevents plaintiffs who sue in federal court from meeting the requirements for standing under Article III of the US Constitution.

they are now at risk of having that information misused to commit future instances of identity theft, fraud, or phishing. Courts have routinely held that this is insufficient to state a claim.[12]

Time and Money Spent Mitigating Risk of Future Harm: Closely related to allegations of a risk of future harm are allegations that plaintiffs expended time or money to mitigate that risk. For example, consumers frequently have alleged harm from the purchase of credit monitoring or identity theft insurance products. However courts have overwhelmingly rejected this theory of injury, finding that such mitigation costs are merely derivative of the speculative risk of future identity theft.[13] A notable outlier is *Anderson v. Hannaford Brothers*, in which an appeals court reversed the dismissal of the plaintiffs' claims under Maine law on the ground that credit monitoring and identity theft insurance products were reasonably foreseeable damages recoverable in negligence.[14] However, *Anderson*'s applicability is likely limited to its very unique facts, as plaintiffs there claimed widespread and ongoing fraud that the defendant conceded was the result of a breach of its systems.[15]

Emotional Injury and Loss of Privacy: Plaintiffs have similarly alleged that the exposure of their information injured them by causing emotional injury, such as anxiety or stress, or a loss of privacy. Neither theory appears to have been embraced by courts. Courts have generally found allegations of emotional distress to be insufficient to state a claim for relief.[16] As to loss of privacy, some courts have held that a loss of privacy constitutes actionable

[12] *See, e.g., Grigsby v. Valve Corp.*, C12–0553JLR , 2012 WL 5993755, at *2 (W.D. Wash. Nov. 14, 2012); *Shafran*, 2008 WL 763177, at *2-3; *see also Krottner*, 406 F. App'x at 131; *Pisciotta v. Old Nat. Bancorp*, 499 F.3d 629, 635, 640 (7th Cir. 2007).

[13] *See Grigsby*, 2012 WL 5993755, at *2; *see also Ruiz v. Gap, Inc.*, 622 F. Supp. 2d 908, 913-6 (N.D. Cal. 2009), *aff'd*, 380 F. App'x 689, 691-92 (9th Cir. 2010); *Belle Chasse Auto. Care, Inc. v. Advanced Auto Parts, Inc.*, CIV.A 08-1568, 2009 WL 799760, at *4-5 (E.D. La. Mar. 24, 2009); *Caudle v. Towers, Perrin, Forster & Crosby, Inc.*, 580 F. Supp. 2d 273, 284 (S.D.N.Y. 2008).

[14] *Anderson*, 659 F.3d at 162–67.

[15] *Id.* at 164 (1st Cir. 2011). As explained below, mitigation damages of the sort sustained in *Hannaford* also are likely not recoverable in federal court under the Supreme Court's recent ruling in *Clapper v. Amnesty Int'l USA*, because "[plaintiffs cannot manufacture [Article III] standing merely by inflicting harm on themselves based on their fears of hypothetical future harm that is not certainly impending." 133 S. Ct. 1138, 1151 (2013).

[16] *See, e.g., Amburgy v. Express Scripts, Inc.*, 671 F. Supp. 2d 1046, 1055 (E.D. Mo. 2009); *In re Hannaford Bros. Co. Customer Data Sec. Breach Litig.*, 613 F. Supp. 2d 108, 132-3 (D. Me. 2009), *aff'd in part, and rev'd in part sub nom. Anderson v. Hannaford Bros Co.*, 659 F.3d 151 (1st Cir. 2011).

harm only if there is an intentional or egregious invasion of privacy not present in actions against breached companies,[17] while others have rejected such claims of harm outright.[18]

Loss of Value of Information: Creative plaintiffs have also attempted to claim that the information they provided to the breached company had some ascertainable economic value, which was diminished by its exposure in the data breach. Courts, however, have consistently rejected the core concept of the theory—that consumer information has any economic value for which a consumer can expect to be compensated.[19] Apart from this defect, courts also have noted that plaintiffs tend to have difficulty demonstrating that a data breach caused any actual diminution in the alleged value of their information.[20] While one decision, *Claridge v. RockYou, Inc.*, allowed a negligence claim to survive a motion to dismiss based on a claim of "los[s] of the value of [information],"[21] it is unlikely to have any persuasive weight at this time. The court stated that the decision was motivated by the "paucity of controlling authority" at that time,[22] and declined to follow it in subsequent cases.[23]

Benefit of the Bargain: Recently, plaintiffs have also claimed injury by alleging that they did not receive the benefit of the bargain with respect to a purchase from the defendants. This theory has met little success thus far. For example, the plaintiffs in *Barnes & Noble* and *In re LinkedIn User Privacy Litig.* each alleged that they paid a premium for the items they purchased from the defendants that was allocated to security of their information.[24] In

---

[17] *See, e.g.*, *Randolph v. ING Life Ins. & Annuity Co.*, 973 A.2d 702, 711 (D.C. 2009); *Ruiz v. Gap, Inc.*, 540 F. Supp. 2d 1121, 1127-28 (N.D. Cal. 2008).

[18] *Hammond v. The Bank of New York Mellon Corp.*, 08 CIV 6060 RMB RLE, 2010 WL 2643307, at *7–8, *11 (S.D.N.Y. June 25, 2010); *Willey v. J.P. Morgan Chase, N.A.*, 09 CIV 1397(CM), 2009 WL 1938987, at *10 (S.D.N.Y. July 7, 2009).

[19] *In re Barnes & Noble Pin Pad Litig.*, 12-CV-8617, 2013 WL 4759588, at *4 (N.D. Ill. Sept. 3, 2013); *In re Jetblue Airways Corp. Privacy Litig.*, 379 F. Supp. 2d 299, 326-7 (E.D.N.Y. 2005).

[20] *LaCourt v. Specific Media, Inc.*, SACV 10-1256-GW JCGX, 2011 WL 1661532, at *4-5 (C.D. Cal. Apr. 28, 2011).

[21] 785 F. Supp. 2d 855, 861, 866 (N.D. Cal. 2011).

[22] *Id.* at 861.

[23] *In re Facebook Privacy Litig.*, C 10-02389 JW, 2011 WL 6176208, at *5 (N.D. Cal. Nov. 22, 2011).

[24] *Barnes & Noble*, 2013 WL 4759588, at *5; *In re LinkedIn User Privacy Litig.*, 932 F. Supp. 2d 1089, 1092 (N.D. Cal. 2013).

each of these cases, the courts dismissed the plaintiffs' claim based on the benefit of the bargain theory as illusory, since the plaintiffs did not allege any defect with the product or service itself, nor any bargain with the defendant for a particular level of security.[25] By comparison, one recent decision denied a motion to dismiss based on the claimed loss of value of computer games sold by the defendant where the plaintiff specifically identified statements in which the defendant allegedly "assured" the plaintiffs that their information would be secure.[26]

Unreimbursed Losses: In contrast to the other theories discussed, plaintiffs are typically able to overcome the injury hurdle if they allege actual misuse of their information resulting in an unreimbursed monetary loss. Consumers who allege having to pay fraudulent charges on their payment cards have been found to satisfy the injury requirement.[27] Significantly, the plaintiff must actually incur the loss that is claimed. For example, it is well-established that a consumer has not suffered any cognizable injury related to a fraudulent credit card charge if that charge was later reimbursed by the card issuer, as often occurs.[28] Further, if an instance of identity theft fails to result in any actual loss to the consumer, there has been no recoverable injury.[29]

Causation of Damages

Apart from the requirement to show cognizable injury, plaintiffs typically must show that the claimed injury was caused by the defendant's actions. In data breach cases, causation is a particularly prominent issue with respect to allegations of actual misuse of a plaintiff's information. A central question with which the court must grapple is what allegations—and later, evidence—is required to show that a particular instance of misuse was perpetrated using data stolen from the breached company. In *Slaughter v. AON Consulting, Inc.*, the court crystallized this issue by dismissing claims for negligence under Delaware law, because the plaintiffs had not provided any reason to believe that the two claimed instances of identity theft "were not the result of

[25] *Id.*
[26] *Grigsby v. Valve Corp.*, 12-CV-00553, slip op. at *8 (W.D. Wash. Mar. 18, 2013).
[27] *In re Michaels Stores Pin Pad Litig.*, 830 F. Supp. 2d 518, 527 (N.D. Ill. 2011).
[28] *Anderson*, 659 F.3d at 155 n.2 (1st Cir. 2011); *In re Michaels Stores*, 830 F. Supp. 2d at 527.
[29] *Krottner*, 406 F. App'x at 131.

something else."[30] By contrast, the Ninth Circuit in *Stollenwerk v. Tri-West Health Care Alliance* found a showing of detailed factual information to support temporal and logical connections between the breach and misuse to be sufficient, in that case, to avoid dismissal at summary judgment.[31] The inability to plead reliance on assurances of security has also been the focus of some cases dismissing for lack of causation.[32]

Limitations under Particular Causes of Action

Finally, damages that would otherwise be recoverable may be prohibited because of principles that are specific to the cause of action the plaintiff is bringing. For instance, defendants in data breach actions often seek dismissal of negligence claims based on the economic loss doctrine.[33] In general, the economic loss doctrine forecloses a purchaser of a product or service from recovering in tort for economic losses without accompanying damage to person or property, and instead requires that any action be brought on a contract theory, if at all.[34] Defendants in data breach cases have achieved success in obtaining dismissal of negligence claims based on the economic loss doctrine under various states' laws.[35] Courts have rejected attempts to argue that the exposure of electronic data, or the destruction (by the plaintiffs) of their credit cards to prevent further fraud, amounted to "property damage" precluding the application of the economic loss doctrine.[36] However, the contours of the economic loss doctrine can vary from state to state, and certain states impose at least some limitations on its application. Given these nuances, data breach defendants have not been uniformly successful in asserting the economic loss doctrine to defeat negligence claims at the motion to dismiss stage.[37]

---

[30] *Slaughter v. AON Consulting, Inc.*, CIV.A. 10C-09-001FSS, 2012 WL 1415772, at *2, *4 (Del. Super. Jan. 31, 2012).

[31] *Stollenwerk v. Tri-W. Health Care Alliance*, 254 F. App'x 664, 668 (9th Cir. 2007) (reversing summary judgment); *see also Resnick v. AvMed, Inc.*, 693 F.3d 1317, 1325-9 (11th Cir. 2012).

[32] *In re LinkedIn*, 932 F. Supp. 2d at 1092.

[33] *Cumis Ins. Soc'y, Inc. v. BJ's Wholesale Club, Inc.*, 918 N.E.2d 36, 46-7 (Mass. 2009).

[34] *Apollo Grp., Inc. v. Avnet, Inc.*, 58 F.3d 477, 480-1 (9th Cir. 1995).

[35] *Cumis*, 918 N.E.2d at 46-7 (holding that Massachusetts law precluded recovery in negligence for economic loss in a data breach case); *Sovereign Bank v. BJ's Wholesale Club, Inc.*, 533 F.3d 162, 175-78 (3d Cir. 2008) (same result under Pennsylvania law).

[36] *In re TJX*, 564 F.3d at 498; *Cumis*, 918 N.E.2d at 46-7.

[37] *See Lone Star Nat'l Bank supra* n. 5; *Merrick Bank Corp.*, 2008 WL 4277877, at *7-8.

Causes of Action Asserted

Even if data security breach plaintiffs allege a sufficient injury causally connected to the defendant's conduct, they must still assert the remaining elements of a valid cause of action. We explain below the claims that are often asserted, as well as how courts have addressed them.

Contract

Plaintiffs frequently assert contract-based theories in data security breach litigation. A plaintiff pressing a breach-of-contract claim must plead and prove:

1. the existence of a binding contract or agreement;
2. the non-breaching party fulfilled its contractual obligations;
3. the breaching party failed to fulfill its contractual obligations without legal excuse; and
4. the non-breaching party suffered damages as a result of the breach.[38]

Plaintiffs in data security cases often claim that the breached company made a contractual promise to protect personal information and breached that obligation.

Setting aside the above-described difficulties involved in showing both the fact and the causation of damages, claimants have in many instances stumbled on the threshold requirement of showing a binding promise by the breached company. For instance, many courts have declined to treat a company's statements about its security practices, such as in a privacy policy, as an enforceable contract.[39] Where a payment card brand claims that a merchant or its acquiring bank agreed to pay fines and assessments for compromising payment card data, one court has suggested that such promises are unenforceable under state law because they are contractual penalties.[40]

In many instances, plaintiffs have sought to address the absence of an express agreement by claiming that the breached company created an "implied"

---

[38] *Rachells v. Cingular Wireless*, 483 F. Supp. 2d 583, 589 (N.D. Ohio 2007).
[39] *See, e.g., In re Zappos.com, Inc.*, 3:12-CV-00325-RCJ, 2013 WL 4830497, at *3 (D. Nev. Sept. 9, 2013); *but see Jetblue Airways*, 379 F. Supp. 2d at 325-26 (treating privacy policy as contract for purposes of motion to dismiss).
[40] *Genesco*, 2013 WL 3790647, at *23.

contract to safeguard data when it collected their personal information. An implied contract typically requires all of the elements of an express contract, except that the parties' assent is manifested through conduct rather than words.[41] In limited circumstances some courts have sustained data security plaintiffs' claims, for purposes of a motion to dismiss, that a merchant from whom they purchased goods or services implicitly agreed to take reasonable measures to protect their information.[42] By contrast, at least one court has rejected such a claim.[43] Courts have routinely dismissed such claims against breached companies with whom the plaintiffs shared no direct relationship, on the ground that absent direct dealings, there is no basis to infer from the parties' conduct mutual asset to contract.[44]

Plaintiffs have also sought to address a lack of a direct relationship with the breached company by claiming they are "third party beneficiaries" of, and thus entitled to enforce, the company's contracts with other parties in which the company promised to safeguard personal information. These claims, however, require the plaintiffs to plead and prove that the contracting parties intended to benefit the plaintiffs through their contract, as opposed to merely conferring a benefit on the plaintiffs incidentally.[45]

Tort

Tort-based theories of liability in data security breach cases typically involve claims for negligence and/or negligent misrepresentation, but can occasionally give rise to other tort claims as well.

Negligence: As noted above, plaintiffs in data breach actions frequently assert negligence claims under the theory that the breached defendant had a duty to exercise reasonable care in protecting the plaintiffs' personal information, and that the defendant breached that duty by failing to establish adequate

[41] *In re Heartland Payment Sys., Inc. Customer Data Security Breach Litig.*, 834 F. Supp. 2d 566, 581 (S.D. Tex. 2011), *rev'd in part sub nom. Lone Star Nat'l Bank, N.A. v. Heartland Payment Sys., Inc.*, 729 F.3d 421 (5th Cir. 2013).

[42] *See, e.g., In re Hannaford Bros.*, 613 F. Supp.2d at 119.

[43] *In re Zappos.com*, 2013 WL 4830497, at *3.

[44] *See, e.g., Willingham v. Global Payments, Inc.*, 1:12-CV-01157-RWS, 2013 WL 440702, at *18 (N.D. Ga. Feb. 5, 2013) (recommending dismissal where consumers and payment processor had no direct relationship).

[45] *Id.* at *20 (recommending dismissal of a claim by consumers that they were third party beneficiaries of a payment processor's contracts with merchants).

safeguards to protect the information and/or by failing to provide timely notification of the breach.[46] To succeed on a negligence claim, plaintiffs typically must show:

1. the existence of a duty to exercise due care,
2. breach of that duty,
3. causation, and
4. damages.[47]

In addition to facing difficulties associated with showing cognizable injury and causation, and with overcoming the economic loss doctrine (as noted above), plaintiffs must also plead and prove the threshold requirement that the defendant owed them a duty of care.[48] Courts have been particularly likely to reject plaintiffs' efforts to meet this requirement where, for example, the plaintiffs and the defendant have no direct relationship,[49] or where the posited duty derives from a statute that does not apply to the facts of the case.[50]

Negligent and/or Intentional Misrepresentation: In addition to negligence claims, plaintiffs in data breach actions frequently assert claims for misrepresentation, claiming that the defendant, whether in its advertising, marketing, privacy policies, or bank contracts, represented that it would take reasonable measures to safeguard customer information.[51] To state a claim for negligent misrepresentation, a plaintiff must allege:

1. that the defendant made a material misrepresentation;
2. with negligence, i.e., without reasonable ground for believing it to be true;
3. that the plaintiff justifiably relied on the statement; and
4. that, as a result of this reliance, the plaintiff suffered injury.[52]

---

[46] *See, e.g.*, *Ruiz v. Gap, Inc.*, 380 F. App'x. 689, 691; *TJX*, 564 F.3d at 498-99.

[47] *Ruiz*, 380 F. App'x. at 691.

[48] *Merrick Bank Corp.*, 2008 WL 4277877, at *11-12 (dismissing negligence claim in data security breach suit for lack of duty).

[49] *Willingham*, 2013 WL 440702, at *18 (a breached payment processor owed no duty to consumers who provided information to third party merchants).

[50] *Id.* (no duty under a statute requiring provision of notice of breach to Georgia residents, where the plaintiffs were not Georgia residents).

[51] *In re TJX*, 564 F.3d at 494.

[52] *Small v. Fritz Companies, Inc.*, 65 P.3d 1255, 1258 (Cal. 2003).

A claim of intentional or fraudulent misrepresentation has similar elements, with a heightened scienter requirement.[53] In addition to prevailing on the damages issues described above, defendants in data breach matters have also succeeded in pressing arguments that plaintiffs failed to demonstrate reasonable or "justifiable" reliance on the alleged misstatement made by the defendant.[54]

Other Tort-Based Theories: Plaintiffs will occasionally proffer other tort-based theories of liability, such as negligence per se, conversion, breach of fiduciary duty, or tortious interference, which have met little success.

Other Common Law Principles

Unjust Enrichment: Unjust enrichment is a quasi-contractual theory of recovery that private litigants have asserted in several recent data breach actions.[55] Although the elements of a claim for unjust enrichment vary by state, a plaintiff must typically at least allege that he or she conferred a benefit on the defendant, the retention of which is unjust.[56] Since a benefit is required, claims for unjust enrichment are ordinarily brought only by data breach plaintiffs who allege having purchased some product or service from the defendant.[57]

Although unjust enrichment provides plaintiffs with an alternative to traditional contract and tort actions, it has its own obstacles that plaintiffs have found difficult to overcome. As a threshold matter, not all states recognize unjust enrichment as a standalone cause of action.[58] Even where

---

[53] *Id.*

[54] *Cumis Ins. Soc'y, Inc. v. BJ's Wholesale Club*, 455 Mass. 458, 471-6 (2009) (affirming summary judgment for defendant because credit unions could not have reasonably relied on any alleged misrepresentations); *see also In re Heartland Payment Sys.*, 834 F. Supp. 2d at 594 (dismissing negligent misrepresentation claim under Rule 12(b)(6) because allegation of reliance was conclusory), *rev'd in part sub nom. Lone Star Nat'l Bank, N.A. v. Heartland Payment Sys., Inc.*, 729 F.3d 421 (5th Cir. 2013).

[55] While this section explores courts' treatment of claims for unjust enrichment, the principles discussed are likely applicable to similar equitable claims, such as restitution or money had and received.

[56] *See, e.g., AMP Servs. Ltd. v. Walanpatrias Found.*, 73 So. 3d 346, 350 (Fla. Dist. Ct. App. 2011); *Hertz Corp. v. RAKS Hospitality, Inc.*, 196 S.W.3d 536, 543 (Mo. Ct. App. 2006); *Martin v. E. Lansing Sch. Dist.*, 483 N.W.2d 656, 661 (Mich. Ct. App. 1992); *R. Zoppo Co., Inc. v. City of Manchester*, 453 A.2d 1311, 1313 (N.H. 1982).

[57] *See, e.g., Bell v. Blizzard Entm't, Inc.*, No. 12-CV-09475 BRO (PJWx), slip op. at *7-8 (C.D. Cal. July 11, 2013) (consumers alleged that a video game developer sold them games, but failed to abide by assurances in its privacy policy).

[58] *See In re Sony Gaming Networks & Customer Data Sec. Breach Litig.*, 903 F. Supp. 2d 942,

unjust enrichment provides a standalone cause of action under state law, it is often unavailable where the plaintiff has an adequate remedy at law or where there is an express contract between the parties that governs the dispute.[59]

Bailment: A more novel claim asserted by plaintiffs in recent years is that the defendant is liable for a data breach as the bailee of plaintiffs' information. Bailment is the relationship that arises when personal property is delivered to another for some particular purpose with an express or implied contract to redeliver the property when the purpose has been fulfilled, or to otherwise deal with the property according to the bailor's instructions.[60] A classic example of bailment is the delivery of a car to a parking attendant.[61]

Though creative, claims for bailment in the data security space have not proven to be viable.[62] For one thing, no court has accepted the proposition that consumer information is "property" of a type that can be bailed.[63] For another, as courts have noted, it is unclear how such information can be "delivered" to companies or "returned" to consumers.[64] Moreover, courts have noted that in the typical data breach action, there is no allegation that the defendant was involved in perpetrating the theft, or that the defendant otherwise sought to deprive plaintiffs of their information.[65] Accordingly, bailment is not a claim likely to benefit most plaintiffs.

State Statutes

In addition to common law claims, data breach plaintiffs frequently assert causes of action under state consumer protection statutes. State by state

---

973-4 (S.D. Cal. 2012) (dismissing an unjust enrichment claim under California law in a data breach case for this reason).

[59] *See, e.g.*, *Bell supra* n. 57 at *8 (citing *BAE Sys. Info. & Elec. Sys. Integration v. Lockheed Martin Corp.*, CIV.A. 3099-VCN, 2009 WL 264088, at *7 (Del. Ch. Feb. 3, 2009)).

[60] *Earhart v. Callan*, 221 F.2d 160, 163 (9th Cir. 1955).

[61] *See* BLACK'S LAW DICTIONARY (9th ed. 2009).

[62] *In re Sony Gaming Networks*, 903 F. Supp. 2d at 974-5; *Ruiz v. Gap, Inc.*, 540 F. Supp. 2d 1121, 1126-7 (N.D. Cal. 2008), *aff'd*, 380 F. App'x 689 (9th Cir. 2010); *Richardson v. DSW, Inc.*, 05 C 4599, 2005 WL 2978755, at *4 (N.D. Ill. Nov. 3, 2005); *Bell*, No. 12-CV-09475, at *15-16.

[63] *See Bell*, No. 12-CV-09475, at *15.

[64] *In re Sony Gaming Networks*, 903 F. Supp. 2d at 974.

[65] *Id.*; *Ruiz*, 540 F. Supp. 2d at 1127.

variations in the requirements under these statutes can exist, but they often proscribe deceptive and/or unfair business practices. Some states also have data breach notification statutes that allow a cause of action for injury flowing from a breach of the statute's requirements. Courts have held data breach plaintiffs proceeding under an "unfairness" theory to a high standard of proof. Specifically, a plaintiff must show that the data security practices were (1) "systematically reckless," (2) "aggravated by [a] failure to give prompt notice," and (3) "cause[d] very widespread and serious harm to…innumerable consumers."[66] Furthermore, courts in data security breach cases have held that certain consumer protection statutes are intended to protect consumers, and thus commercial entities such as issuing banks are not proper plaintiffs under these statutes.[67]

Federal Statutes

Fair Credit Reporting Act: Private litigants have also brought claims against companies that suffer data security breaches pursuant to the Fair Credit Reporting Act (FCRA),[68] but a number of courts have dismissed such claims at the pleading stage.

The Fair Credit Reporting Act creates obligations on three types of parties: (1) consumer reporting agencies,[69] (2) furnishers of credit information to consumer credit reporting agencies,[70] and (3) users of consumer credit reports.[71] Recent data security breach cases have tended to involve claims relating to the FCRA's provisions governing consumer reporting agencies. Such claims frequently involve two threshold issues: (1) whether the company that was subject to the data security breach falls under the definition of a consumer reporting agency, and (2) whether the company violated the FCRA's requirement that such an agency establish "reasonable procedures designed to…limit the furnishing of consumer reports to the purposes" permitted by the statute.[72] Plaintiffs have faced an uphill battle

---

[66] *See In re Michaels Stores*, 830 F. Supp. 2d 518, 526 (N.D. Ill. 2011) (citing *In re TJX*, 564 F.3d at 496).
[67] *See, e.g., In re Heartland Payment Sys.*, 834 F. Supp. 2d at 605-07.
[68] 15 U.S.C. §§ 1681 *et seq*. (West).
[69] 15 U.S.C. § 1681e.
[70] 15 U.S.C. § 1681s-2.
[71] 15 U.S.C. § 1681m.
[72] *See* 15 U.S.C § 1681e(a).

characterizing a breached company as a "consumer reporting agency" subject to the statute, which courts have typically limited to those entities traditionally understood to be the three major credit reporting bureaus—Experian, Equifax, and TransUnion.[73] Other courts have grounded their dismissals on the plaintiffs' failure to demonstrate that the defendant creates "consumer reports" as opposed to merely handling payment or other consumer information.[74] Courts have also rejected plaintiffs' arguments that the plaintiffs' data was "furnished" for purposes of the statute, holding that allegations of theft cannot be construed as "furnishing" a consumer report.[75]

Other Federal Statutes: In addition, data breach plaintiffs occasionally bring actions under other federal statutes, including sections of the Electronic Communications Privacy Act (ECPA),[76] commonly referred to as the Wiretap Act. Although actual damages are not required to state a claim under certain provisions of the Wiretap Act,[77] actions under this provision are brought infrequently because, to state a claim, a plaintiff must allege that the defendant engaged in the intentional interception, disclosure, or use of data or communications in violation of the Wiretap Act.[78] Similarly, data breach plaintiffs occasionally assert claims for violation of the Stored Communications Act (SCA),[79] the section of the ECPA barring providers of certain communication services from divulging private communications to third parties; however, such claims have also been unsuccessful to date.[80]

Data security-related suits by shareholders under securities statutes have likewise been infrequent, because such shareholders face difficulty pleading

[73] *See, e.g.*, *Holmes v. Countrywide Fin. Corp.*, 5:08-CV-00205-R, 2012 WL 2873892, at *15 (W.D. Ky. July 12, 2012); *F.T.C. v. Gill*, 265 F.3d 944, 948 (9th Cir. 2001).

[74] *Fuges v. Sw. Fin. Servs., Ltd.*, 707 F.3d 241, 252-5 (3d Cir. 2012); *Willingham*, 2013 WL 440702, at *13-14 (Mag. Judge's Final Report and Recommendation); *Garnett v. Millennium Med. Mgmt. Res., Inc.*, 10 C 3317, 2010 WL 5140055, at *2-3 (N.D. Ill. Dec. 9, 2010).

[75] *Holmes*, 2012 WL 2873892, at *16.

[76] 18 U.S.C. §§ 2510–22 (West).

[77] *See* 18 U.S.C. § 2520(c)(2).

[78] *See* 18 U.S.C. §§ 2511(1)(a), (c) & (d).

[79] 18 U.S.C. §§ 2701–11 (West).

[80] *See, e.g.*, *In re Michaels Stores*, 830 F. Supp. 2d at 523-5 (holding that the craft retailer did not provide "electronic communication services" or "remote computing services," as necessary to state a claim under the SCA).

and proving that the breached company made material misstatements or omissions about its security practices, that it did so with the requisite scienter, and that the alleged misrepresentations or omissions caused losses to the shareholders.[81]

Procedural Issues

Article III Standing

Data breach plaintiffs seeking to invoke federal jurisdiction must satisfy the standing requirements of Article III of the United States Constitution. Specifically, a plaintiff must show an injury-in-fact that is "(a) concrete and particularized" and "(b) actual or imminent, not conjectural or hypothetical."[82] Further, plaintiffs must demonstrate that the claimed injury is fairly traceable to the conduct complained of.[83]

Constitutional standing has emerged as a prominent issue in the data security space, as it addresses the core issue in the practice discussed above: whether plaintiffs have suffered any actual injury as a result of the breach. In the rare instance where plaintiffs claim actual misuse of the information compromised in the breach, there is little doubt that plaintiffs satisfy Article III's injury-in-fact requirement.[84] Conversely, courts agree that plaintiffs fall short of establishing any injury-in-fact where they cannot show that their information was compromised.[85] Where plaintiffs' allegations of injury fall between these two extremes—such as where plaintiffs claim harm from the mere exposure of their information during a data breach—the courts have split.[86]

---

[81] *See In re Heartland Payment Sys. Inc. Sec. Litig.*, CIV. 09-01043, 2009 WL 4798148, at *3-8 (D. N.J. Dec. 7, 2009) (dismissing a shareholder federal securities suit because the plaintiffs failed to plead material misstatements and scienter); *In re Choicepoint, Inc. Sec. Litig.*, No. 05-00686, slip op. at 6-9 (N.D. Ga. July 21, 2008) (despite having initially denied the defendant's motion to dismiss, approving settlement in part because of a significant risk that the plaintiffs would fail to prove material misstatements or omissions, scienter, and loss causation).

[82] *Lujan v. Defenders of Wildlife*, 504 U.S. 555, 560 (1992) (internal citations omitted).

[83] *Id.*

[84] *See, e.g.*, *Lambert v. Hartman*, 517 F.3d 433, 437 (6th Cir. 2008).

[85] *Katz v. Pershing, LLC*, 672 F.3d 64, 79 (1st Cir. 2012); *Hammer v. Sam's East, Inc.*, 12-CV-2618-CM, 2013 WL 3756573, at *3 (D. Kan. July 16, 2013).

[86] *Compare, e.g.*, *Reilly v. Ceridian Corp.*, 664 F.3d 38, 45 (3d Cir. 2011) (no standing), *with Pisciotta*, 499 F.3d at 634 (standing satisfied).

However, a recent decision by the United States Supreme Court appears to have resolved this split in favor of the courts finding a lack of standing. In *Clapper v. Amnesty International USA*, the Supreme Court dismissed for lack of standing a suit brought by attorneys and organizers who alleged that their communications were likely to be monitored under a purportedly unconstitutional federal surveillance statute, given that they worked with persons likely to be targeted for surveillance.[87] Although the dispute in *Clapper* did not involve a data breach, the decision's potential implications for the data security space are clear. For one, the Court expressly rejected the proposition that an "objectively reasonable likelihood" of harm can suffice for standing, instead holding that the threatened harm must be "certainly impending."[88] Further, the Court's rejection of standing based on a "speculative chain of possibilities" in *Clapper* is closely analogous to the Third Circuit's reasoning in *Reilly* that speculation as to a hacker's intent or ability to commit identity theft does not create standing.[89] Finally, two federal district courts have already applied the *Clapper* decision in the data breach context, in each case dismissing the plaintiffs' complaint for lack of standing.[90] Accordingly, although the full weight of the Supreme Court's decision in *Clapper* has yet to be felt, it appears that the door to the federal courthouse may be closing for plaintiffs who are unable to allege actual misuse of their information.

Federal courts hearing data security breach cases have also been largely unreceptive to other theories of standing. For example, plaintiffs have claimed harm from time and money spent mitigating the purported risk of identity theft, such as for credit monitoring services. However, the Supreme Court's decision in *Clapper* appears to have foreclosed that theory as well.[91] Plaintiffs have also asserted injury from a purported diminution in the economic value of their information, but numerous courts have dismissed such claims on Article III standing grounds.[92] With

---

[87] *Clapper*, 133 S. Ct. at 1148-50.

[88] *Id.* at 1143.

[89] *Compare Clapper*, 133 S. Ct. at 1148-50 *with Reilly*, 664 F.3d at 45.

[90] *See Barnes & Noble*, 2013 WL 4759588, at *5 (speculation as to the risk of identity theft is insufficient under *Clapper*); *Hammer*, 2013 WL 3756573, at *2-3.

[91] *See Barnes & Noble*, 2013 WL 4759588, at *4; *Clapper*, 113 S. Ct. at 1151 ("[Plaintiffs] cannot manufacture standing merely by inflicting harm on themselves based on their fears of hypothetical future harm that is not certainly impending.").

[92] *Barnes & Noble*, 2013 WL 4759588, at *5; *In re iPhone App. Litig.*, No. 11-02250, 2011

respect to claims of generalized anxiety or stress, courts in particular contexts have reached differing conclusions as to whether such injuries are sufficient to confer standing,[93] but *Clapper* suggests that such theories will be rejected going forward.[94] Finally, plaintiffs have also had mixed results in alleging injury-in-fact from their failure to receive the benefit of the bargain.[95] Where the claim is misrepresentation-based, however, this theory has been held not to suffice to establish standing absent an allegation that the plaintiffs actually read the purported misrepresentations regarding the defendant's security practices.[96]

Class Certification

Plaintiffs in data security breach cases often seek to bring litigation as a class action. However, such plaintiffs face significant challenges in obtaining certification of a class. When seeking certification in federal court under Federal Rule of Civil Procedure 23, the burden is on the representative plaintiffs to show that the prerequisites of Rule 23(a)—numerosity, commonality, typicality, and adequacy—are satisfied. In addition, the representative plaintiffs must provide evidentiary proof that "questions of law or fact common to class members predominate over any questions affecting only individual members, and that a class action is superior to other available methods for fairly and efficiently adjudicating the controversy."[97] As clarified by the Supreme Court in 2011, this is more than a "mere pleading standard."[98] In fact, trial courts addressing the issue are instructed to conduct a "rigorous analysis."[99] As a result, courts frequently deny class certification in data breach litigation.

In particular, even where data security breach plaintiffs are able to satisfy the requirements of Rule 23(a), Rule 23(b) has proven to be a significant obstacle

---

WL 4403963, *4-5 (N.D. Cal. Sept. 20, 2011); *LaCourt v. Specific Media, Inc.*, No. 10-1256, 2011 WL 2473399, at *4-5 (C.D. Cal. Apr. 28, 2011); *but see also Claridge*, 785 F. Supp. 2d at 861.

[93] *Compare Krottner*, 628 F.3d at 1142 (sufficient), *with Reilly*, 664 F.3d at 44-45 (insufficient).

[94] *Clapper*, 113 S. Ct. at 1151.

[95] *Compare Grigsby*, No. 12-CV-00553, slip op. at *8 (allowing standing) *with Barnes & Noble*, 2013 WL 4759588, at *5 (denying standing) *and In re LinkedIn*, 2013 WL 844291, *4 (same).

[96] *In re LinkedIn*, 2013 WL 844291, at *4.

[97] *See* FED. R. CIV. P. 23(b)(3).

[98] *Wal-Mart Stores, Inc. v. Dukes*, 131 S. Ct. 2541, 2551 (2011).

[99] *Id.*

to class certification.[100] Rule 23(b)(3) permits class certification only if "the court finds that the questions of law or fact common to class members predominate over any questions affecting only individual members."[101] However, data breach litigation claims are often based on individual issues of causation and damages. To establish misrepresentation, for instance, plaintiffs must prove reliance on an inaccurate representation (or omission). Even when uniform misrepresentations are made to potential class members, the plaintiffs' reactions to the defendant's misrepresentation could, and likely will, differ. As one court explained, proving reliance "will necessarily involve individual questions of fact."[102] In data breach litigation particularly, there is a strong argument that some plaintiffs did not rely on the alleged misrepresentation when deciding to provide personal information.

Similarly, plaintiffs have a difficult time arguing that fraud losses are consistent across the class. In a recent data security breach case decided on the issue of predominance, *In re Hannaford Bros. Co. Customer Data Sec. Breach Litigation*, customers' credit and debit card information was stolen from a grocery store.[103] The court noted that questions relating to the company's conduct were common to the class, but the actual impact of the data breach varied from plaintiff to plaintiff: "where things differ is in the actual impact on particular cardholders…and the actual mitigating steps they took and the costs they incurred."[104] The court ultimately denied certification because the plaintiffs had not presented any expert testimony demonstrating that total damages incurred by the putative class could be proven by statistical methods.[105] Likewise, *In re TJX* ruled that the predominance requirement was not met because losses that result from or are related to fraudulent transactions could not be demonstrated on a classwide basis, "[g]iven that there are a myriad of ways in which fraud losses can occur, as well as the fact that the plaintiffs themselves have admitted the difficulty of attributing any particular loss to the data breach."[106]

---

[100] A class may also be certified if it meets any of the three requirements of 23(b). However, b(1) and b(2) classes rarely arise in data breach litigation and are therefore not addressed in this chapter.
[101] FED. R. CIV. P. 23(b)(3).
[102] *In re TJX Cos. Retail Sec. Breach Litig.*, 246 F.R.D 389, 395 (D. Mass. 2007).
[103] *In re Hannaford Bros. Co. Customer Data Sec. Breach Litig.*, 2:08-MD-1954-DBH, 2013 WL 1182733, *1 (D. Me. Mar. 20, 2013).
[104] *Id.* at *8.
[105] *Id.* at *9-10.
[106] *In re TJX Companies*, 246 F.R.D. at 397.

Claims for Indemnification by the Breached Company

While thus far we have focused on claims against a corporate victim of a data security breach, it also bears noting that such a company is not necessarily without recourse to recoup losses it suffers by reason of the breach. Such companies sometimes seek indemnification from third parties, such as from service providers or technology suppliers that allegedly were at fault for the breach, or insurers that allegedly issued policies covering the losses resulting from the breach.

Few such suits have drawn judicial opinions, but those that have suggest that at least some viable claims can be pressed by breach victims. A recent decision permitted a suit against a provider of technology and related services to proceed to trial in federal court.[107] There, restaurant chain Cotton Patch Cafe (Cotton Patch) sued payment processing equipment provider Micros Systems, Inc. (Micros) over alleged deficiencies in a Micros payment processing system that purportedly caused a payment card data breach at one of Cotton Patch's restaurants in Nacogdoches, Texas, requiring the restaurant to pay over $250,000 in fines and assessments imposed by Visa and MasterCard.[108] Cotton Patch sued Micros for damages in the US District Court for the District of Maryland, asserting claims for violation of Texas's Deceptive Trade Practices Act, negligence, negligent misrepresentation, gross negligence, and fraud by nondisclosure.[109] The court granted summary judgment to Micros on Cotton Patch's claims for negligence and gross negligence under Texas law based on the economic loss doctrine, but denied Micros's motion for summary judgment on the restaurant's claims under the Deceptive Trade Practices Act and for negligent misrepresentation and fraud by nondisclosure.[110] As to the misrepresentation and fraud claims, the court reasoned that there were genuine issues of material fact as to whether Micros misrepresented or withheld information regarding security deficiencies in the payment processing system.[111] On the Deceptive Trade Practices Act claim, the court reasoned that there were

---

107 *Cotton Patch Cafe, Inc. v. Micros Sys., Inc.*, CIV.A. MJG-09-03242, 2012 WL 5986773 (D. Md. Nov. 27, 2012).
108 *Id.* at *2.
109 *Id.* at *3.
110 *Id.* at *9.
111 *Id.* at *7-8.

genuine issues of material fact as to whether Cotton Patch was a "consumer" entitled to protection under the statute.[112] The parties tried the case before a jury for two days, and then settled the dispute and stipulated to a full dismissal.[113]

In addition, at least one decision has sustained a claim by a breached company against an insurer. Recently, the US Court of Appeals for the Sixth Circuit affirmed summary judgment in favor of a data security breach victim, DSW Shoe and certain related companies, against an insurer that contested coverage of losses DSW suffered from a data security breach in which hackers stole customer payment card information from the retailer's computer network.[114] DSW had "incurred expenses for customer communications, public relations, customer claims and lawsuits, and attorney fees" in connection with investigations by government agencies, as well as assessments imposed by the credit card brands.[115] The Sixth Circuit affirmed summary judgment for DSW on the ground that its losses were covered under an insurance policy that covered "[l]oss which the Insured shall sustain resulting directly from…[t]he theft of any Insured property by Computer Fraud."[116]

Conclusion

As the above discussion demonstrates, even accepting the prevailing wisdom that every company has or will at some point be victimized by a data breach, and must incur significant legal, customer relations, and other costs as a result, far from every such company will be held legally responsible to private litigants. Courts are often hesitant to open their doors to redress the types of intangible or speculative harm (if any) that such breaches frequently create, and in any event, a company's being victimized by a data security breach does not necessarily mean it has breached its legal obligations. As plaintiffs continue to press claims over data security breaches, practitioners in this area should closely watch for further developments in this continuously evolving area of the law.

---

[112] *Id.* at *8-9.
[113] Joint Stipulation of Dismissal with Prejudice (filed Sept. 4, 2013).
[114] *Retail Ventures, Inc. v. Nat'l Union Fire Ins. Co. of Pittsburgh, Pa.*, 691 F.3d 821 (6th Cir. 2012).
[115] *Id.* at 824.
[116] *Id.* at 827, 831-4.

Key Takeaways

- Make clients who have suffered a data security breach aware that they may face claims by a variety of private litigants, such as the individual or individuals whose data was potentially stolen or at risk of being stolen, issuing banks and payment card brands (if payment card data was potentially compromised), or shareholders.
- In defending private data security breach litigation, focus especially on issues surrounding lack of cognizable injury and damages to the plaintiff, as courts are often hesitant to open their doors to redress the types of intangible or speculative harm (if any) that data security breaches frequently create.
- Keep in mind that a company's being victimized by a data security breach does not necessarily mean it has breached its legal obligations.
- When advising a corporate victim of a data security breach, remind the client to review the potential for seeking indemnification from third parties, such as insurers.
- Watch for further developments in this continuously evolving area of the law to properly advise clients as plaintiffs continue to press claims over data security breaches.

Douglas H. Meal, a partner at Ropes & Gray LLP, represents companies in complex transaction-related disputes arising from all varieties of business agreements. Most recently, Mr. Meal has played a leading role in the firm's privacy and data security practice, specializing particularly in representing clients targeted by litigation and government investigations stemming from highly publicized data security breaches. As the lead outside lawyer handling claims stemming from the data security breaches suffered by Sony, Heartland Payment Systems, The TJX Companies, Nationwide, Hannaford Brothers, Aldo, Genesco, and Wyndham Hotels—some of the most highly publicized data security breaches in recent years—Mr. Meal has become the national leader in defending companies that suffer significant data security breaches involving consumer information against the ensuing claims and regulatory investigations.

Acknowledgment: *I thank my assistant author, associate David Cohen in Ropes & Gray LLP's Washington, DC office. Mr. Cohen, whose practice focuses on complex business and commercial disputes, has extensive experience working with corporate clients* *that have suffered data security breaches or have been accused of privacy violations, defending them against class actions and claims asserted by payment card brands, and representing them in connection with federal and state government investigations. I also thank the other Ropes & Gray LLP associates who contributed to the content and research for this chapter, including Sunil Shenoi, Lisa Rachlin, Dan Routh, and Joseph Cleemann.*

Assisting Clients with Cybersecurity and the Protection of PII and PHI

Phyllis B. Sumner

Partner

King & Spalding LLP

ASPATORE

Introduction

The security of personal identifying information (PII), protected health information (PHI), and company proprietary and sensitive information is of significant concern to individuals, companies, and government agencies in the US and globally. As companies struggle to protect such information and to comply with expanding legal requirements, the threat of cybercrimes continues to grow. Cybersecurity is now a top priority for the Executive and Legislative branches of government, as well as top of mind for executives and boards of public and private companies. To combat this threat and comply with evolving and expanding legal requirements, companies should periodically assess and update their privacy policies and information security programs. When appropriate, companies also should share threat information and cooperate with law enforcement.

Key Trends in Privacy and Data Security in the US

The cybersecurity of personal and sensitive data is a key trend. Federal lawmakers continue to focus on potential legislation to federalize security incident response and data breach notification requirements. This increasing focus stems from the high number of cyberhacking and other security incidents among US companies. Even President Obama has focused on the threat of cybersecurity to our national security.

On February 12, 2013, President Obama issued Executive Order 13636, "Improving Critical Infrastructure Cybersecurity."[1] The Executive Order calls for the development of a voluntary Cybersecurity Framework that provides a "prioritized, flexible, repeatable, performance-based, and cost-effective approach" for assisting organizations responsible for critical infrastructure services to manage cybersecurity risk. The Executive Order tasked the National Institute of Standards and Technology (NIST) with leading the creation of the Cybersecurity Framework. Once the Framework is established, the Department of Homeland Security (DHS) will establish a voluntary program to support adoption of the Framework by owners and operators of critical infrastructure.

[1] Exec. Order 13636, Improving Critical Infrastructure Cybersecurity, 78 Fed. Reg. 11,737 (Feb. 12, 2013).

On February 26, 2013, NIST published a Request for Information (RFI) in the Federal Register soliciting views from both government and industry on developing the Cybersecurity Framework. The Framework will consist of standards, methodologies, procedures, and processes that align policy, business, and technological approaches to address cyber risks.

NIST's RFI sought information related to the protection of "critical infrastructure" in three areas:

1. The use of frameworks, standards, guidelines, and best practices;
2. Current risk management practices within industry; and
3. Specific industry practices.

The RFI defined "critical infrastructure" to mean "systems and assets, whether physical or virtual, so vital to the US that the incapacity or destruction of such systems and assets would have a debilitating impact on security, energy, national economic banking security, national health care, public health, or safety and transportation."[2]

NIST's questions focused on risk assessment and how cybersecurity factors into that risk assessment, as well as the current usage of various frameworks and standards.

The RFI also sought to understand "the current regulatory and regulatory reporting requirements in the US (e.g., local, state, national, and other) for organizations relating to cybersecurity" and what occurs where an organization is required to report to more than one regulatory body and what resulting information must be reported under these current regulations.[3] Stakeholders were required to provide comments on the RFI to NIST by April 5, 2013.

On October 22, 2013, NIST released its Preliminary Cybersecurity Framework.[4] The framework was designed to help critical infrastructure

---

[2] Developing a Framework to Improve Critical Infrastructure Cybersecurity, 78 Fed. Reg. 13,024 (Feb. 26, 2013).
[3] *Id.*
[4] Improving Critical Infrastructure Cybersecurity Executive Order 13636 Preliminary Cybersecurity Framework, *available at* http://www.nist.gov/itl/upload/preliminary-cybersecurity-framework.pdf.

owners and operators reduce cybersecurity risks in industries such as power generation, transportation and telecommunications. NIST issued a forty-five-day public comment period and plans to issue the official framework in February 2014. The Framework was developed in collaboration with industry and provides guidance and best practices to organizations on managing cybersecurity risk. A key objective of the Framework is to encourage organizations to prioritize cybersecurity risks, much like organizations prioritize financial, safety and operational risk. NIST will use the comment period to determine whether its proposed standards, best practices, and guidelines will meaningfully improve security of critical infrastructure.

Congressional and executive branch interest in these issues is increasing, and could generate significant pressure for industry adoption of those voluntary standards.

If there is a congressional effort to establish some level of mandatory standards, it is likely that those would be based to a large degree on the voluntary standards developed by NIST.

Impacts on Key US Industries and Companies

Cybersecurity impacts not only the defense industrial base, but also providers of banking, energy, transportation, health care, Internet, and e-commerce services. Such industries are the lifeblood of our country and the infiltration, exfiltration, and destruction of critical data could significantly impact our economy and national security. Again, the increase in the number of cyber attacks as well as the level of sophistication of cyberhacking continues to grow and pose a significant threat.

The risks associated with inadequate data security controls have bubbled up to the board level in many companies. As board members question their general counsels and other business stakeholders about the security of sensitive company data, many companies are unable to answer questions such as: what sensitive information do we maintain? Where do we maintain it? Who has access to it and how do we protect it?

Information technology (IT) departments are frequently undergoing security assessments and penetration testing to uncover network and application weaknesses and exploitable vulnerabilities to security threats. Industry best practices, along with several federal and state laws, require organizations to review their information systems and security measures frequently—and at least annually—to combat the risk of ever-evolving cybersecurity threats.

Legislation Impacting Privacy

No major federal legislative provisions relating to cybersecurity have been enacted since 2002, despite many recommendations made over the past decade. The Obama Administration sent Congress a package of legislative proposals in May 2011. Cybersecurity legislation advanced in both chambers in the 112th Congress. The House passed a series of bills that address a variety of issues, from toughening law enforcement of cybercrimes to lessening liability for private companies that adopt cybersecurity "best practices." The Senate pursued a comprehensive cybersecurity bill, but to no avail.

Four issues caused conflict between the House and Senate versions of the legislation:

(1) requirements on critical infrastructure (mandatory or voluntary standards);
(2) the scope of new authority for information sharing between industry and government;
(3) government use of information after it is received; and
(4) the degree of liability protection.

Most observers believe Congress will let President Obama's Executive Order on critical infrastructure play out.

The following chart lists the Senate and House legislation under consideration in the 113th Congress:

Major Legislation: Senate			
S. 21	Cybersecurity and American Cyber Competitiveness Act of 2013	Homeland Security and Government Affairs	January 22, 2013
S. 1638	Cyber Security Public Awareness Act of 2013	Homeland Security and Government Affairs	October 31, 2013

Major Legislation: House			
H.R. 86	Cybersecurity Education Enhancement Act of 2013	Education and the Workforce; Homeland Security; Science, Space, and Technology	January 3, 2013
H.R. 624	Cyber Intelligence Sharing and Protection Act (CISPA)	Permanent Select Committee on Intelligence	February 13, 2013
H.R. 756	Cybersecurity R&D	Science, Space, and Technology	February 15, 2013
H.R. 1121	Cyber Privacy Fortification Act of 2013	Judiciary	March 13, 2013
H.R. 967	Advancing America's Networking and Information Technology Research and Development Act of 2013	Science, Space, and Technology	March 14, 2013
H.R. 1163	Federal Information Security Amendments Act of 2013	Oversight & Government Reform	March 14, 2013
H.R. 756	Cybersecurity Enhancement Act of 2013	Science, Space, and Technology	April 16, 2013

The debate over whether a national data security breach notification law should be implemented has been ongoing over the last decade. Issues including whether a national law should preempt state laws—along with debates over what types of information should be subject to breach notification rules and how long companies have before reporting the breaches—has held up a national breach notification bill for years.

Debates regarding the scope and reach of cybersecurity laws also are issues that have held up many proposed laws in that area. Recent legislative developments include several cybersecurity bills that have advanced in the House. On April 16, 2013, the House passed the Federal Information Security Amendments Act of 2013, which amended the Federal Information Security Management Act (FISMA) of 2002 to reestablish oversight authority of the Director of the Office of Management and Budget (OMB) with respect to agency information and security policies and procedures.

In May 2013, the House also passed the Cybersecurity Enhancement Act of 2013, and Advancing America's Networking and Information Technology Research and Development Act of 2013.[5] Both of these bills are aimed at increasing research for cybersecurity and information technology issues. The House Permanent Select Committee on Intelligence passed the Cyber Intelligence Sharing and Protection Act (CISPA) (information sharing and liability protection). CISPA would allow for sharing of Internet traffic information between the US government and technology and manufacturing companies. The intent of the bill is to help the US government investigate cyber threats and to ensure critical infrastructure from cyber attacks. The White House issued a veto threat citing privacy concerns.

State Data Privacy Laws

Most companies that conduct multi-state business or whose customers reside in multiple states recognize the need to comply with multiple state laws concerning privacy and data security. California enacted the first data breach notification law in 2002.[6] Currently forty-six states, the District of Columbia, Guam, Puerto Rico, and the Virgin Islands have enacted data breach notification laws. The four states that have not enacted breach notification laws are Alabama, Kentucky, New Mexico, and South Dakota.

Notification and compliance with the state data breach notification laws is increasingly difficult for businesses that have a national presence. For example, if a database containing personal identifying information was breached in California, but contained information related to residents of thirty-five other states, the data owner needs to comply with the data breach notification laws of all thirty-five states.[7] While most state data breach notification laws contain similar elements, important differences exist. Below highlights some of the variations among state data breach notification laws.

---

[5] H.R. 756, 113th Cong. (2013); H.R. 967, 113th Cong. (2013-14).

[6] SB 1386 (Ca. 2003); Ann. Cal. Civ. Code §§ 1798.82 & 1798.29 (West).

[7] The Texas data breach notification law requires notification to affected Texas residents and residents of any other state that does not have its own data breach notification law. In other words, if a database in Texas is breached and that database contained personal information of Alabama residents, the residents of Alabama would need to be notified in accordance with the Texas data breach notification law because Alabama does not have its own data breach notification law.

Personal Information. One of the first questions to ask in the event of a data security incident is whether the data involves personal information, which triggers state data breach notification laws. The typical definition of personal information includes an individual's name (usually first name and first initial and last name) and at least one other piece of identifying information, such as a social security number, driver's license number, state identification card, or credit card number. A growing number of states have expanded the traditional definition of personal information. For example, Iowa,[8] Wisconsin,[9] and Nebraska[10] include biometric data, Maryland[11] includes an individual taxpayer identification number, Oregon[12] includes a passport number, and Wyoming[13] includes a tribal identification card in their definitions of "personal information." California recently passed new legislation that will take effect in January 2014, which expands the definition of personal information to include a user name or e-mail address in combination with a password or security question and answer that would permit access to an online account.[14] As states continue to look to California for guidance with data security regulations, additional states will likely adopt California's expanded definition of "personal information."

Notification Obligation. States vary in their identification of the triggers that require notification. Many states require notification if personal information "was, or is reasonably believed to have been" obtained by an unauthorized person, regardless of the likelihood that the consumer will be a victim of identity theft or fraud.[15] Other states permit companies to evaluate the risk of harm to consumers and require notice only if it is "reasonably likely" that the unauthorized access will result in identity theft or fraud.[16]

Method of Notification. The mode by which organizations can notify consumers of a breach also varies by state. By and large, most states permit notification via mail or e-mail, but notification by e-mail must comply with the Federal

---

[8] Iowa Code Ann. § 715C.1 (2008).
[9] Wis. Stat. Ann. § 134.98 (2008).
[10] Neb. Rev. Stat. § 87-802 (West).
[11] Md. Code Ann. § 14-3501 (2008).
[12] Or. Rev. Stat. § 646A.602(11)(a)(C).
[13] Wyo. Stat. § 40-12-501 (West).
[14] S.B. 46 (Ca. 2013).
[15] *See* Cal. Civ. Code § 1798.82; Fla. Stat. Ann. § 817.5681 (2005); Ga. Code Ann. § 10-1-912 (2007).
[16] *See* Del. Code Ann. tit. 6 § 12B-102 (West); Ind. Code Ann. § 24-4.9-3-1 (2009).

Electronic Signatures Act, 15 U.S.C. § 7001, which requires companies seeking to use e-mail notice to obtain affirmative consumer consent. Almost all states, with the exception of Utah, permit substitute notice if the number of affected individuals exceeds a certain number or if the cost of notice exceeds a certain amount. The substitute notice typically involves publishing the notice in widely distributed state media and on the company's website.

Timing of Notification. Most state data breach notification laws require notification to the affected consumers "in the most expedient time possible and without unreasonable delay," while others prescribe a specific period of time within which notification must be made.[17] Most state laws allow for delayed notification consistent with the legitimate needs of law enforcement, but note, that some states, such as Illinois,[18] require law enforcement to provide a written request for delay.

Content of Notification. Some state breach notification laws contain required content for the notice, while others do not specify any content requirements.[19] The content requirements can make it difficult to send a uniform notice to all affected residents because some state laws require contact information of the state attorney general.[20]

Additional Parties to Notify. In addition to notifying the affected consumers, many state data breach notification laws require notification to state entities, such as the state attorney general. In New York, for example, a breach notification form must be sent to the New York Division of State Police, the New York State Attorney General's Office, and the New York Department of State.[21]

---

[17] *Compare* Cal. Civ. Code § 1798.82 ("The disclosure shall be made in the most expedient time possible and without unreasonable delay…") *with* Fla. Stat. § 817.5681 ("Notification must be made no later than 45 days following the determination of the breach…").

[18] 815 Ill. Comp. Stat. Ann. 530/10 (West).

[19] Examples of states with notification content requirements: Cal. Civ. Code § 1798.29; Mass. Gen. Laws 93H § 3 (2007); 815 Ill. Comp. Stat. Ann. § 530/10; Md. Code Ann. § 14-3504; Mich. Comp. Laws Ann. § 445.72; N.C. Gen. Stat. Ann. § 75-65 (2009); N.Y. Gen. Bus. Law § 899-aa (2013). Examples of states with no notification content requirements: Del. Code Ann. tit. 6 § 12B-102; Fla. Stat. Ann. § 817.5681; Ga. Code Ann. § 10-1-912; Ind. Code Rev. 24-4.9-3-1; Mont. Code Ann. § 30-14-1704 (West); N.J. Stat. Ann. § 56:8-163 (2006); Ohio Rev. Code Ann. § 1349.19 (2007); Okla. Stat. Ann. tit. 24 § 163 (West); Pa. Stat. Ann. § 2303; Tenn. Code Ann. § 47-18-2107 (2008); Tex. Bus. & Com. Code § 521.053 (2013); Wash. Rev. Code § 19.255.001.

[20] *See* Md. Code Ann. § 14-3504; N.C. Gen. Stat. Ann. § 75-65.

[21] N.Y. Gen. Bus. Law § 899-aa.

Most states that require notification to a state agency have data breach reporting forms on their websites. In addition, some states require notification to the national consumer reporting agencies. Notification to consumer reporting agencies is commonly triggered only if a certain number of individuals are affected. In Florida, the national consumer reporting agencies need to be notified if more than 1,000 individuals are affected by the breach.[22]

Due to the disparity among state data breach notification laws and the absence of a unifying federal law, companies that operate across multiple states typically seek to comply with the most restrictive laws (which often are in California). This golden standard approach generally is more practical and efficient than developing a state-specific patchwork of policies and procedures. It is important, however, to periodically assess state data breach notification laws as they frequently change. Companies should ensure they have experienced counsel to assist them in identifying the relevant breach notification laws and preparing compliant notifications. It is recommended to have attorneys with relevant experience included in the company's incident response plan so that the research and planning for notification can occur quickly and concurrently with the breach investigation.

New PHI Compliance Concerns

While some industries are scrambling to catch up with state and federal privacy and data security requirements, HIPAA "covered entity" health care providers and health plans and their direct "business associate" vendors have for some time been tuned in to their obligations to protect Protected Health Information (PHI). As the reach of the Health Insurance Portability and Accountability Act of 1996 (HIPAA) expands, however, other industries that collect, handle, or maintain PHI are facing significant new obligations. For example, second-tier downstream vendors of HIPAA covered entities must now comply with HIPAA.

The definition of "business associate" applies to any individual or entity that:

> on behalf of such covered entity...but other than in the capacity of a member of the workforce of such covered entity or arrangement, creates, receives, maintains, or transmits

[22] Fla. Stat. § 817.5681.

> protected health information…or who provides, other than in the capacity of a member of the workforce of such entity, legal, actuarial, accounting, consulting, data aggregation…, management, administrative, accreditation, or financial services…where the provision of the service involves the disclosures of protected health information from such covered entity or arrangement.[23]

The new HIPAA/Health Information Technology for Economic and Clinical Health (HITECH) regulations, which required compliance effective September 23, 2013, expanded the definition of "business associate" (BA) to include a "subcontractor" that creates, receives, maintains, or transmits PHI on behalf of a business associate. "Subcontractor" is defined to mean a person "to whom a business associate delegates a function, activity, or service, other than in the capacity of a member of the workforce of such business associate."[24]

Covered entities must obtain "satisfactory assurances" from BAs—except from a subcontractor. The BAs are responsible for obtaining satisfactory assurances from subcontractors.

Three potential arguments weigh against BA status for a particular "person":

(1) their inclusion in the covered entity's workforce (the workforce exception);
(2) their exposure to PHI is "incidental or inadvertent" (the janitor or workman exception); or
(3) they are a "mere conduit" of the information, taking it from one "place" to another (the UPS or postal exception).

The Office for Civil Rights (OCR), Department of Health and Human Services (HHS) describes the conduit theory as a "narrow" exception limited to transmission and temporary storage of data incident to transmission, with random or infrequent access to PHI. The OCR focuses on the "transient versus persistent" nature of that opportunity.

---

[23] Modifications to the HIPAA Privacy Rules, 78 Fed. Reg. 5,566, 5,572 (Jan. 25, 2013); 45 C.F.R. pt. 160.103.

[24] 78 Fed. Reg. at 5,572; 45 C.F.R. pt. 160.103.

According to the OCR, the conduit theory can apply to broadband suppliers and Internet Service Providers, but not to document storage companies. The OCR has specifically modified the BA definition to add the word "maintains"—to clarify this interpretation.

BAs now face direct liability for impermissible uses and disclosures. The OCR recognizes that "[a]ny privacy rule limitation on how a covered entity (CE) may use or disclose PHI automatically extends to a BA."[25]

BAs have exposure for:

- Failure to provide breach notification to a CE;
- Failure to provide access to ePHI to the CE, individual, or the individual's designee, as necessary to fulfill the CE's obligations;
- Failure to use or disclose PHI consistent with the business associate obligations set forth in the privacy rule;
- Failure to comply with the security rule; and
- Failure to furnish the HHS Secretary with information when required for investigation of HIPAA compliance.

Despite this expansion of liability, except as described above, there is no direct application of all of the privacy rule to BAs. CEs, of course, are subject to all of the requirements of the privacy rule, including to:

- Provide a notice of privacy practices;
- Designate a privacy official;
- Establish policies and procedures (required for BAs under the security rule); and
- Furnish access to individuals' health and billing records and amend those records upon request in appropriate circumstances.

HITECH also focused on breach notification. It directed HHS to issue regulations regarding a CE's obligation to notify individuals of a breach of their unsecured PHI, and regarding a BA's obligation to notify the CE of a breach. Prior to HITECH, HIPAA contained no breach notification requirements.

[25] *Id.* at 5,597.

Pursuant to HITECH, certain notifications must be made by CEs (and BAs) in the event of a "breach":

(1) acquisition, access, use, or disclosure in a manner not permitted under the privacy rule (impermissible use/disclosure);
(2) of unsecured PHI; and
(3) that "compromises the security or privacy of the PHI."

Prior to the final HITECH regulations, the "harm" standard applied (i.e., poses a significant risk of financial, reputational, or other harm to the individual). Now, an impermissible use/disclosure is "presumed to be a breach" unless the CE or BA demonstrates that there is "a low probability that the protected health information has been compromised based on a risk assessment"[26] of at least four factors. The risk assessment factors include:

(1) the nature and extent of the PHI involved, including the types of identifiers;
(2) the unauthorized person who used the PHI or to whom the disclosure was made;
(3) whether the PHI was actually acquired or viewed; and
(4) the extent to which the risk to the PHI has been mitigated.

Each of the four factors must be addressed, and other factors may be addressed. The risk assessment must be thorough and in "good faith." Alternatively, the CE or BA may decide to simply provide notice without conducting a risk assessment. Notification may be avoided altogether if the information is properly encrypted and therefore no longer is "unsecured PHI." OCR "encourages" CEs and BAs to take advantage of the safe harbor for encrypted information.

Changing Practices in Response to Changing Laws: BA Agreements

In response to recent changes in this area, Business Associate Agreements, which set forth vendor HIPAA obligations, are now common practice. Further, CEs and BAs are developing incident response plans that incorporate HIPAA/HITECH and state disclosure law requirements.

---

[26] *Id.* at 5,695.

BA Agreements should include:

(1) The BA is not in compliance with the privacy rule if the BA knew of a pattern/practice of subcontractor breach/violations, unless the BA takes reasonable steps to cure a breach, end a violation, or terminate, if feasible.
(2) The BA will comply with the security rule.
(3) The BA will report breaches of unsecured PHI.
(4) The BA will ensure that subcontractors agree to the same restrictions and conditions.
(5) If the BA is required to perform the CE's privacy rule obligations, the BA must comply with privacy rule requirements applicable to the CE.

BA Agreements are necessary to:

- Clarify and limit appropriate uses and disclosures;
- Impose contractual obligations for actions for which there is no direct liability;
- Notify the BA of regulated status; and
- Clarify responsibilities, such as how to handle an individual's request for access received directly by the BA.

The HITECH omnibus regulations required compliance by September 23, 2013, including as applicable to new business associate contracting requirements. However, existing agreements may be "grandfathered" for up to a year. To be eligible for grandfathering:

- An entity must have a compliant BA or "downstream" agreement in place prior to January 25, 2013; and
- The agreement was not renewed or modified from March 26, 2013 to September 23, 2013.[27]

If eligible for grandfathering, compliance is required on the first to occur of: September 22, 2014 or the date the contract is renewed or modified on or after September 23, 2013.

[27] *Id.* at 5,569-70.

Attorneys should provide proactive advice to assist clients in developing compliant BA agreements and incident response plans. It is key to widely distribute incident response plans across the organization so that all employees are aware of the appropriate procedures in the event of a security incident and to immediately inform the proper individuals. Attorneys should provide reactive counseling to assist clients in the event of a security incident. In addition, it is often necessary to engage a technology firm to perform forensic analysis to determine the extent and root cause of a potential breach. It is important to react quickly, but equally important to assess whether a reportable breach occurred prior to notifying consumers. Often times, forensic analysis may show that a data breach did not result in any unauthorized access to data (for example, if the data was properly encrypted) such that notification is not required. With the tight reporting time for a data breach under HIPAA and some state laws, however, these determinations need to be made quickly. It is important to have a team ready to act if and when a security incident occurs.

Global Developments in Privacy and Data Security

Like the US, the EU is focused on privacy and cybersecurity issues. The European Union Data Protection Directive[28] was adopted in 1995 and went into effect in 1998. The Directive requires each member state of the EU to adopt privacy regulations and governs the protection of individual privacy rights and processing and transfer of personal data. The Directive imposes strict requirements on the collection and processing of personal data. The Directive permits transfer of personal data within the EU to member states, but it strictly regulates transfers of data outside the EU. Data transfers outside the EU are not permitted unless the other jurisdiction offers an "adequate level of protection" or another basis for transfer exists. The United States has not been deemed to have an adequate level of protection, so to transfer data from the EU to the United States, the parties must implement model contracts, comply with binding corporate rules, or apply for a Safe Harbor. Entities that agree to participate in the Safe Harbor promise to apply fair information practices, as set forth in the Safe Harbor framework. The Safe Harbor process is an annual certification with the Department of Commerce. The FTC and the Department of Transportation enforce the Safe Harbor

[28] Directive 95/46/EC (E.U. 1995).

provision. The European Counsel is currently considering whether Safe Harbor is fit for purpose in the current data environment or whether the regime should be overhauled following the NSA/Prism disclosures.

On January 25, 2012, the European Commission released the Data Protection Regulation. The adoption is aimed for 2014 and the regulation is planned to take effect in 2015. The new Regulation proposes significant fines for non-compliance, including up to 2 percent of the organization's revenue or €1 million. European Council discussions regarding the specific contents of the Regulation are still ongoing but the likely changes include:

- A wider definition of "personal data";
- The need for explicit consent to process personal data;
- The requirement to appoint a Data Protection Officer for large organizations;
- Giving individuals the right to be forgotten and the right to ask old service providers to transfer their personal data to new service providers;
- Removal of the requirement to register with European data protection authorities; and
- The requirement to report data breaches within twenty-four hours.

If and when the Regulation is adopted, it will likely have an important impact on data protection requirements within and outside the EU.

The EU also is focused on cybersecurity issues. The European Commission established the European Cybercrime Center (EC3) at Europol (European law enforcement agency) at The Hague. EC3 was mandated to tackle online fraud and cybercrime affecting critical infrastructure and information systems.

EC3's strategy and prevention system includes:

- Analysis of data to understand how fraudsters operate;
- Helping law enforcement agencies target operations more effectively;
- Monitoring developments in emerging technologies;
- Informing policy and legal changes;
- Advising citizens and businesses to protect against online threats; and

- Leading Project 2020—a strategic foresight initiative for the International Cybersecurity Protection Alliance on the future of cybercrime.

Other countries around the world are active in the privacy area as well. Canada, for example, has a comprehensive data privacy law like the EU, the Personal Information Protection and Electronic Documents Act of 2000 (PIPEDA). PIPEDA applies to every organization that collects, uses or discloses personal information in the course of commercial activities. PIPEDA prohibits an organization from using personal information without the person's consent except in certain situations, including law enforcement investigations and emergencies. Other examples of privacy laws are listed below:

Argentine Personal Data Protection Law	France's Data Processing, Data Files and Individual Liberties Act
German Federal Data Protection Act	South Korean Personal Data Protection Act
Columbian Law 1266/08	Australian Privacy Act
Japan's Act on the Protection of Personal Information	Austrian Data Protection Act
Chilean Personal Data Protection Act	Hungary Data Protection Act of 2011
India's Information Technology Rules	Mexico's Data Protection Law
Spanish Data Protection Act	Russian Personal Data Law
Indonesia's Electronic Information and Transaction Law	Czech Data Protection Law

As companies become increasingly global, it is imperative to understand how data is used and transferred within the organization. Reviewing the laws of all of the countries where the company does business is imperative for a comprehensive international compliance program. Counsel can assist organizations to develop a compliance plan. Some countries' legal requirements may conflict with laws or obligations elsewhere. One common example of conflicting requirements is when a company needs to rectify its legal e-discovery obligations in the United States with data transfer restriction laws in other countries. Counsel can assist clients make difficult compliance decisions by considering the potential risk involved with non-compliance and factors such as the uncertain regulatory state of a country's privacy laws and, in some circumstances, the limited enforcement of the privacy laws by governing bodies.

Effective Strategies for Adhering to Applicable Laws and Regulations

With the myriad of federal, state, and international privacy and information security laws, it can be a daunting task for companies to determine all of its legal obligations. The first step toward compliance is to assess all types of data the company collects, where that data is processed and stored, and whether that data is transferred. This is a critical step in determining the organization's legal obligations and needs to be updated regularly to account for changing business practices. Legal obligations may be effectively assessed only after the organization knows where it collects, processes, stores, and transfers data.

It also is important for companies to continuously assess whether there is a valid business purpose to collect and maintain certain data. Most companies can eliminate significant exposure simply by assessing whether certain data collections are necessary, and, if they are necessary, whether it is necessary for the organization to maintain that data.

Helping Clients Focus their Data Management and Data Security Efforts

Before prioritizing data security efforts, it is important for a company to take stock of the types of data it collects, handles, and maintains and to determine if it is necessary to continue to do so. Once the company determines the types of data it must continue to handle, then the company should categorize that data and identify the current security protecting such data. Certain levels of security are legally required, and others are driven by the company's desire to protect its data assets.

Once a company establishes an adequate inventory of sensitive data, then it should review the five major categories of information system controls to assess security:

(1) Access controls;
(2) Configuration management controls;

(3) Segregation of duties;
(4) Continuity of operations planning; and
(5) Information Security Programs.

Top Strategies for Helping Clients Respond to a Data Security Breach

The top strategies for responding to a data security breach include: timely reaction; thorough and credible forensic analysis; effective remediation; evaluation of legal obligations, such as data breach notifications; and a strong public relations strategy. Having a dedicated response team poised to respond and mobilize quickly is the key to a successful breach response. Following a breach response, it is important for the client to implement any additional remediation steps that will assist in preventing similar breaches in the future and to thoroughly document all steps that were taken during the breach response process. In addition, after the dust settles, it is important to take a step back to review the process and implement any necessary changes to enhance and strengthen breach preparedness.

Conclusion

As the electronic collection, transfer and maintenance of PII and PHI continue to expand so do the ways to breach security. As a result, state, federal and international laws continue to evolve to protect consumers. Unfortunately, the laws are not always consistent and their reach may depend on many factors, including the type of business, geographic location of the business, and the state or country of residence of their customers. Lawyers in this practice area must stay abreast of changing laws and industry standards to advise their clients on the most practical and legally compliant ways to combat cybersecurity and to protect PII and PHI.

Key Takeaways

- Advise clients to assess the types of data they collect, process, maintain, and transfer to determine their legal obligations under the myriad of state, federal, and international privacy laws. Clients should evaluate whether the data they collect is necessary for a valid business purpose, and if so, whether there is a business need to retain such data.

- Once a company determines the types of data it must collect and retain, it should categorize that data and identify the current security protecting such data so that counsel can analyze whether the company's policies and procedures are compliant with legal requirements.
- Assist clients by developing new, or reviewing and updating existing, privacy policies and Information Security Programs and by ensuring that they have adequate incident response plans.
- Provide proactive advice to assist clients in developing and enforcing compliant BA agreements.
- Provide reactive counseling to assist clients in the event of a security incident.
- Inform clients that the top strategies for responding to a data security breach include: timely reaction; thorough and credible forensic analysis; effective remediation; evaluation of legal obligations, such as data breach notifications; and a strong public relations strategy.

Phyllis B. Sumner is a partner in King & Spalding LLP's Business Litigation Practice Group in Atlanta. She represents clients in a wide variety of complex litigation matters involving privacy and information security, commercial disputes, False Claims Act, Fair Credit Reporting Act, RICO, securities and fraud, and provides counsel on a variety of corporate matters, including privacy and information security compliance, white-collar criminal and regulatory enforcement matters and internal corporate investigations. She also regularly advises clients who experience security incidents and subsequent investigations and litigation.

Ms. Sumner served as an Assistant United States Attorney, first for the Northern District of Illinois and then for the Northern District of Georgia, where she successfully prosecuted public corruption, domestic terrorism, tax, financial fraud, identity theft, money laundering, healthcare fraud and other complex criminal matters. She has extensive experience handling complex, high-profile matters, including the cases against Centennial Olympic Park bomber, Eric Rudolph, and former Mayor of Atlanta, Bill Campbell. She has tried a significant number of federal jury trials, directed numerous grand jury investigations and litigated hundreds of evidentiary hearings. Ms. Sumner applies her extensive trial and prosecutorial experience to the representation of clients in civil and criminal litigation, as well as internal and government investigations.

Acknowledgment: *I would like to acknowledge Sarah E. Statz, senior associate at King & Spalding LLP, who is my right hand on privacy and information security matters, for her research and capable assistance drafting this chapter. I also would like to acknowledge two of my partners, with whom I consult on a regular basis. I would like to thank Robert M. Keenan, for his guidance regarding HIPAA/HITECH, and Pulina Whitaker, for her guidance regarding global data security.*

ASPATORE

Avicenna On Medicine and Its Topics

Adapted By

Laleh Bakhtiar

From Translations by

O. Cameron Gruner and Mazar H. Shah

Correlated with the Arabic by Jay R. Crook

with Notes by O. Cameron Gruner

Great Books of the Islamic World, Inc.

Printed in the United States of America.

Library of Congress Cataloging-in-Publication Data

Ibn Sina, Abu Ali al-Husayn ibn Abd Allah
The Canon of Medicine (al-Qanun fi'l tibb)
Lecture 1 - On Medicine and Its Topics
1. Islam. 2. Medicine. I, Title

ISBN 10 (Book): 1-56744-986-7
ISBN 13 (Book): 978-1-56744-986-0
ISBN 10 (eBook): 1-56744-987-5
ISBN 13 (eBook): 978-1-56744-987-7

Cover Design by Liaquat Ali
Cornerstones are Allah and Muhammad connected by *Bismillah al-Rahman al-Rahim* (In the Name of God, the Merciful, the Compassionate).

Design and layout by Abir Usman

Published by
Great Books of the Islamic World, Inc.

Distributed by
KAZI Publications, Inc.
3023 W. Belmont Avenue
Chicago IL 60618
Tel: 773-267-7001; FAX: 773-267-7002
email: info@kazi.org